Out Live, Out Laugh, Out Love

by

Tina Wesson

For booking information contact:

Owen Entertainment
1708 21st Avenue S. #274
Nashville, TN 37212

Info@OwenEntertainment.com

Bloomington, IN Milton Keynes, UK

AuthorHouse™
1663 Liberty Drive, Suite 200
Bloomington, IN 47403
www.authorhouse.com
Phone: 1-800-839-8640

AuthorHouse™ UK Ltd.
500 Avebury Boulevard
Central Milton Keynes, MK9 2BE
www.authorhouse.co.uk
Phone: 08001974150

First published by AuthorHouse 9/5/2006

ISBN: 1-4259-4057-9 (sc)
ISBN: 1-4259-4058-7 (dj)

Printed in the United States of America
Bloomington, Indiana

This book is printed on acid-free paper.

Cover photo credit: Charlie Brooks

☙ Dedication ❧

I would like to dedicate this book to , Dale. It is because of him that this book has come to life. He always encouraged me and believed that there was a book inside of me that needed to be written. His sense of pride in me is unmatched and unwavering. Thank you, Dale, for everything.

I would also like to thank my parents, Jim and Carolyn, for giving me a chance in life. Had it not been for you, I am sure there would not be a book, and possibly not even a life. Thank you for giving me a chance in this world.

To my children, Katie and Taylor, who remain my happy thought every single day. What would I do without you?

I would be amiss to stop there, for it is only by God's great mercy and grace that I am here with a story to tell. May He be glorified and feel loved by one of His children through this effort.

C3 Acknowledgments 80

Cindy Owen - Your work ethic both inspires and tires me! Thank you for helping me make this book a reality.

Jim McClusky, Chuck Swindoll, Rick Dunn and Doug Banister, Brennan Manning - You never know when you are touching a life!

~ In memory of Roma, Vicki, and Robbie ~

It is a mistake not to live all you can.

⚘ FOREWORD ⚘

I have been hounded for years to write a book. Time is such a valuable commodity in my life that I feel like I would be committing a crime to take up someone's precious time unless I had a story to amaze, a life to inspire, or humor to lighten the load of the reader. For whatever reason, my gift (or curse at times) seems to be that I live with such urgency. Maybe it was my years of working with physically challenged folks, or maybe it was my brush with being stuck in a life that I am not sure I would have survived. Whatever it was, I live my life day by day, as if this just may be my last day here. I ask myself every day, are you living your life to its fullest, and is there anything you need to change in order to do that? Also, I was shown such mercy and grace by my heavenly Father that I am on a mission to love others in the same fashion. These two aspects of my life have brought a meaning and purpose to me that is a guiding star and a certainty in an uncertain world.

I have chosen to give you a little background into my life and then share with you, the reader, some devotionals that had their origins in my personal journals, which I have kept over the years. I tweaked them a bit, adding applicable scripture verses, and I offer them now as a sweet prayer for us all to consider. I am only one voice speaking on behalf of my own personal experiences. It is a little scary writing a spiritual book, because then you are certain to offend someone, because we are all as diverse in our beliefs, as we are in our taste for ice cream. Also, if you write something spiritual in nature, you are some how expected to live an exemplary life. So before you read one word further, I would like to let it be known that I am a mere human with a heart to love and a desire to help my fellow man along the journey. I am certainly no Mother Teresa or Tennessee Williams.

I wanted this book to be something that represented my life and me, but also a book that other people could relate to. So hopefully, somewhere within these pages, you will learn something about me and maybe even find something that the two of us have in common. I also hope that the words you read will help to encourage anyone who may be having a tough time on the journey. We all go through times in our lives that are somewhat unpleasant or difficult, and if there is someone around to cheer you on to face another day, it somehow lightens the load.

I also wanted this book to be a truthful reflection about life. I believe that life has a rhythm and that rhythm is never predictable. Right now, even as I write this, I have attended the celebration of a wedding and then grieved as I drove by a neighbor's house, knowing their teenage son was just killed in a horrible accident. It reminded me that all over the world today, there are people who are joyously dancing to a beat so lively and fun, while there are others who are under the spell of a dull, pounding drum that seems to be losing its beat altogether.

In Ecclesiastes 3:1, the wise King Solomon says it best: *"There is a time for everything, and a season for every activity under heaven."* He goes on to list all the different seasons in life. *"A time to be born and die, plant and uproot, kill and heal, to weep and laugh, to mourn and dance, a time to love and hate, even a time for war and peace."* If there is one thing I know for certain, it is that no one escapes this journey. So as we go through life and experience all the ups and downs that we are destined to have, how can we best go through them with the most grace? How can we face the cruel winds and not let them blow us off balance, or worse still, become bitter? How can we reach out to someone when we really want to knock his or her block off? How can we share our joy with others instead of hogging it all to ourselves?

It is my goal in life to be a good human. I want God to look down from his throne and be pleased that He created me. I want to love the people of my world with the same love that he has shown me. I want to do the best I can, knowing that I have limited human capabilities. That means I do not beat myself up when I fall short of perfection.

I would love to be a pleasing aroma to God, be the best mom on the planet, a caring daughter, and the very best friend one could have. But I have learned to be content with doing the best I can. I do make the effort to try, and I choose to believe others who share this planet with me are doing the same. By doing that, I see the people of my world as pilgrims on the same journey as myself. Each of us set out with dreams of grandeur, hoping for brighter tomorrows.

As long as we are constantly growing as individuals and trying to live in harmony with our fellow man, I think we are doing just fine. The hard part comes in letting that be enough.

I hope you find a glimpse of God in His glory somewhere in these pages. I believe that He is there. I am just the messenger, and you the receiver of His love. God bless you all!

To understand any living thing, you must creep within and feel the beating of its heart. -W. Macneile Dixon

ᙣ Growing Up ᙦ

I do not remember anything about my life before my adoption, which took place when I was three years old. The years that followed, however, are rich with memories, adventures, and a life fully lived.

I was adopted into a home where I reigned as a princess for five wonderful years. My dad would come home from work and he would lie on his back on the floor with his feet up in the air. I would go over and sit on his feet, and he would catapult me across the room. My mom dressed me up like I was her little baby doll. While my dad was teaching me to be a tomboy by playing with snakes and catching crawdads in the creek behind my house, my mom was busy teaching me to be a good Southern woman by buying me an Easy-Bake Oven to teach me how to cook. She would teach me to count using pinto beans, and she was my hero when she held her hands behind her back and told me to pick a hand. Behind her back she held two Tootsie Pops—one for her and one for me. It didn't really matter which one I picked. If I wanted the one she got, she would gladly give it to me, just like she always gave me the most tender part of the steak, or when sharing the spaghetti plate, I got the biggest share.

I had white hair that grew down to my waist, and I was always full of way too much energy. I was my mom's sidekick. We did everything together until I started school. It was then my parents decided (without asking me, I might mention) to get me a baby brother.

I have always said adoption is like Mr. Gump's box of chocolates. You never know what you are going to get. To my good fortune, I am sure my parents were unaware at the time they said yes to taking me in that they were getting a headstrong, independent tomboy of a girl. It could have been at the time of my new baby brother's arrival that my parents realized what might be in store for them in the future. My mom was trying to get me to bond with this little beast that invaded my territory uninvited. In an attempt to break down my displeasure, one day she asked me if I would like to feed my new baby brother, and my reply was curt and to the point: "You bought him; you feed him."

I firmly believe that parents cannot take full credit or blame in the outcome of their children; however, I do believe that as children, we will strive to achieve for ourselves the things we admire about our parents. From my dad, I learned the power behind acceptance. He has always known who I was and loved this little girl just as I am. I never had to change or do anything better or more to win his favor.

My mother loved her family with every fiber of her being. We were not just her job but also her passion. My mom was always waiting for me with a snack when I got home from school. She was the mother of all room mothers. My friends always thought she was the bomb, not just because she was so beautiful, but also because she was creative in party planning and took such interest in all the kids.

My dear mother must have been cursed to have me and my little brother for her children. She is the girliest girl I have ever known. She is femininity times ten. Her nails, hair, and clothes were always perfect! The problem comes from the fact that she took in a little girl who was the biggest tomboy ever and then adopted a little boy who turned out to be extremely hyperactive. I would love to spend the next few pages here telling you stories about my brother. That would include tales of tearing the shingles off the roof, putting bubbles in the gas tank of a neighbor's car, burying dead animals in the sandbox, having rotten cotton removed from his nasal cavity (on more than one occasion), and being in the hospital something like four times in three months before he was two years old. This would all be written just to entertain you, but maybe one day my mom will share those stories with you when she writes *her* book about raising hyperactive children.

My brother and I never walked anywhere—we ran. We never quietly made an entrance—we barged. We lived in a split-level house until I started college, and I don't remember my brother ever walking down the stairs. He either ran, jumped, or slid down them on his tailbone his entire youth. My poor mother never stood a chance! How my mom made it through our formative years I will never know. We challenged her on every level, and I am sure we almost cost her her religion.

Some of my favorite memories from my youth include coming home from school and changing my clothes, then taking off for a hike up the ridge behind our house. I have always enjoyed being in the woods, and I spent a portion of my time alone just hiking.

I laugh at all the good times my best friend Sonya and I had together. We grew up a few houses apart and we were inseparable. We played Cinderella, caught crawdads from the creek, listened to music, went through boys, and basically grew up together. She has been my friend now for forty years, and what a sweet blessing she has been. I am now watching my childhood friend assume the role of caregiver for her mother, who has Alzheimer's. I have been impressed with her level of caring and commitment to her family.

I used to love spending the night with my friend Colleen. She was a tomboy like me and she lived on a farm full of animals to play with. Since she was Catholic, she had as many siblings as she did pets. We would get up early in the morning with the dew still on the ground and the sun just coming up. We would put the reins on the horses and ride bareback over to the train tracks and race the train. I felt like the Lone Ranger, or at least the faithful friend, Tonto. Colleen was a talkative gal, and in seventh grade she was to blame for both of us having to write one hundred times, *"I shall refrain from obnoxious and distracting behavior in social studies class."* I do not know whether to thank her or Mr. Ashworth for teaching me how to spell *obnoxious*.

Some of my fondest memories are of long days at the lake, playing so hard with my friend Tracy. We would go to bed exhausted by the end of the day. That girl matched my energy level, and it was hard to wear us both out. We ended up dating and marrying brothers, and had one day hoped to live next door to each other. The boys were *way* too smart for that! They kept us a few miles apart for everyone's safety.

I had *great* friends in my youth, and I was blessed with such a happy childhood. As an adult, I have found it more difficult to develop long-lasting relationships, so my old faithful friends remain very important to me.

I started my athletic way of life early on. I joined a swim team when I was seven years old. I swam every summer thereafter until I graduated from high school. We were fortunate enough to live right behind the swimming pool, so I would just walk to practice. Practice started at 8 o'clock, so it was chilly in the morning. In between sets, I would warm myself up on the concrete decking. I would be very cold because I was always very skinny. My poor bathing suit would be picked to death from the rough surface. But I loved swimming. I would come home after practice and eat a bowl of Cream of Wheat. Then I would head right back down to the pool for the entire day and then stay for our evening practice after the pool closed. I eventually got a job lifeguarding and teaching swimming lessons, if you want to call that a job.

One of my favorite activities came from swinging on any one of the three grapevines we had close to our house. I loved swinging on those vines like Johnny Weissmuller did in the old Tarzan movies. Looking back, I realize how fearless we were swinging far from safety on these accidents-waiting-to-happen.

I had a Halloween party my eighth-grade year. It was at this party that I introduced my best friend to the grapevine experience. It was an experience that I am sure she regrets. Nancy Gorgous fell several feet with the vine trailing behind her, and she landed on her back across a log in the gully.

The rescue folks had to climb up the mountain with Nancy on the stretcher with a broken back. Nancy spent the rest of her eighth grade year in a body cast from the waist up. She broke her back, but thankfully, she healed up nicely (ah, youth). Our friendship, however, was hampered because our moms decided that the time we spent together should be limited, due to the fact that one of us always seemed to get hurt when we were allowed to play together. That was probably another wise choice my mom made in trying to see to it that I lived long enough to see adulthood.

My next-door neighbor, Tommy Martin, was the victim of the second grapevine. He was in high school when his 6'5" frame came tumbling down—not over a gully but over the road. The best I can remember, he broke his ribs and collarbone. That was enough for the parents to get together and cut the third vine down before anyone else got hurt.

As you can see, I was not the type to be content being indoors playing with dolls. As a matter of fact, that was something that my mom said I never did. I did not sit inside and read or do much of anything indoors, except sleep. Nothing about that has changed as I have aged. I have always attacked life with a vengeance! It has not been any problem for me to exemplify the motto "it is a mistake not to live all you can." I am telling you I am trying! It has always been full speed ahead for me. It was not enough for me to ride around in my dad's golf cart. No, I had to sneak it out and jump hills and ride it through the dirt bike trails. Thank goodness my parents had enough wisdom to say "absolutely not" when I asked for a dirt bike as a preteen. They knew I had one speed and that was *wide open!*

By the time I was sixteen, my parents' "no" would not be so easily accepted. When I had to have my driver's license on my sixteenth birthday, they could not deny their daughter her rite of passage; or maybe they knew my persistence would be relentless until they gave in. One year and six wrecks later, I finally began to harness some of this energy that drives me. My poor parents. They deserve a medal. I may not have given them much to worry about as far as getting into trouble, but I more than made up for it in my zeal for living. My mom never went to sleep unless I was at home safe in my bed.

I love life! I always have. I try to get all that I possibly can out of a day. I manage my time like a taskmaster. You would be hard-pressed to ever find me at home "chilling." For me, napping is not an option; nor is it appealing. I simply cannot sleep if the sun is out calling me. And heaven forbid I should need to get up in the middle of the night and go to the restroom. Unfortunately, my mind is as active as my body. It is often hard to get my mind to shut up and go back to sleep once I wake up.

When I was in high school, I was too busy playing to really care much about having a boyfriend. It wasn't until I was in college that I got serious with a boy. I did date some, but mostly the guys were just good friends.

I did not really know how to treat boys early on. I was into that "punching them on the shoulder" thing. I didn't have a clue how to flirt, but boy could I wrestle! Even now, sometimes I catch myself when I am in the presence of a man; my way of building a relationship involves harassing him or giving him a hard time about something. Some things never change, I guess.

My high school days were a blast. I had the best group of friends. I cannot remember many weekends, if any, when I wasn't spending the night somewhere or someone was spending the night with me. My mother was so gracious to realize that she had a social butterfly living under her roof, and she let me stretch my wings.

I participated in swimming, track, and tennis in high school. I was captain of the swim team and was offered a position on the University of Tennessee swim team but turned it down for several reasons. I played number-one position on the tennis team, and I really wish I had stuck with that sport a little longer and more seriously. I set the school record in the 110 low hurdles, but track was not my favorite sport. The track coach, however, was a very handsome Olympic athlete, so I ran *whatever* he told me to run.

Clubs were important to me while I was in school. I would go to school early for prayer breakfast. I was active in the Fellowship of Christian Athletes as well. Both of these organizations were instrumental in providing me a wonderful group of friends to be accountable to. I thought my job in school was to be nice to everyone. I tried to say hello to everyone. Geeks and freaks, hoods and jocks were all the stereotypical labels that were part of my school. I just saw people. I didn't get very involved in their lives, but I was respectful of them as people. Even today, I try to see everyone as a person and not label him or her or put people into some category. I am trying to impress this on my children, and I feel they are doing a good job following suit.

I went into the field of recreation in college. I am sure my parents were thrilled about spending thousands of dollars to send their daughter to college to learn how to play. However, after I won the biggest game show in history, they have quit their grumbling.

College life at the University of Tennessee was the best! I had a roommate who was a pistol. She was a blonde bombshell who had a disposition to die for. She was my match: Mary Sunshine times two. I don't think anyone else could have lived with us. We were a double dose of *too much!* Together we laughed, went to games, and played intramural sports. We even won the all-intramural sports trophy. At night we became the disco queens, hitting the clubs together. She was a good girl, and we still are such good friends.

My years in college matured me somewhat. I chose a major that I loved: therapeutic recreation. I found a boy I fell in love with and got engaged to. I was involved in Fellowship of Christian Athletes and Campus Crusade for Christ. I made a couple of spring break trips to the beach and learned what college life was all about. I loved the freedom to come and go as I pleased. I loved being my own person. I never felt the need to drink or do drugs. I could have the absolute best time with my friends without needing to have a substance to help me or enhance the moment. I was living high on life without putting things into my body. If a person can learn to find contentment in him- or herself, then that person is going to be less likely to look for it in something external.

I graduated in 1993 and moved to Atlanta, Georgia to be a flight attendant for Eastern Airlines. I spent a year living with two other gals in an apartment, yet we never saw each other. My job was great for a people person like me. I always loved traveling, and this job gave me the ability to spend my four days off going to San Juan or any number of other places I wanted to go.

Being goal-oriented, I was growing restless in my job and was ready to move on to the next phase of my life. This is when I learned the meaning of putting the cart before the horse. I wanted to get married, and I set my sights to do just that. You can read about the joys of that phase in the chapter entitled "Divorce."

I have bought a getaway home tucked away in the mountains of North Carolina, and I have found that to be my peace. I sit on my porch in the mornings with a cup of hot chocolate and watch the hummingbirds attack my feeders. I look out over the lake and I say my prayers of thanksgiving for having such a blessed and wonderful life. God has really outdone Himself for me. I can hardly contain all the blessings He has bestowed upon me.

I must be honest; it is a little difficult for me being in this wonderful place. I am so used to being Little Miss Worker Bee. I am quickly learning to adjust to my new place in life. I thank God every single day for His blessings and His goodness. I feel so fortunate to be where I am and seriously cannot think of one reason not to wake up in a good mood every day of my life.

The important thing is this: to be ready at any given moment to sacrifice what we are for what we could become.-Charles Dubois.

When we feel compassion, we take the shape of that which we see. We understand a thing, we can hold its form, feel its weight, see its color, hear its sound, and know its mind—grow within its heart. We think as poets and understand as angels.

ೞ My Adoption ಬ

It is amazing to me that God has been so good to me. At forty-five years of age, I can now look back over my life and see how God's mighty hand was moving and preparing this wonderful plan for me. I guess that is why the verse Jeremiah 29:11 has such a special meaning for me in my life. The verse states, *"For I know the plans I have for you declares the Lord. Plans to prosper you, not to harm you. Plans to give you a hope and a future."* That plan, which included hope and a future, started when I was a little girl. I was born Danette Nicely. I was the youngest of five children at the time. The family struggled financially and the father had a drinking problem at the time. From information I have been given, I know that both the father and the mother struggled to take care of us children. By the time I was about a year and a half old, there was no father or mother at home to care for us. My older brothers wanted to keep all of us kids together and they did everything they could to do just that. They were burning leaves in the oven for heat and tried to shoot birds out of the trees to give us something to eat. My big sister took care of me like I was her personal baby doll. Not wanting to dwell too much on the hardships, I will go on to say that it all proved just too difficult for the kids to overcome. I am very glad that I don't have a memory of any of those details. I really cannot imagine all that my siblings had to endure. My heart aches for their past.

It was finally decided that help was needed in order for us to survive. There was nothing to eat, and we knew something had to be done.

Somehow, some way, my grandparents were contacted and they stepped in and took all of the children. They were apparently old and to care for five children would be quite a task, especially when there was a toddler involved. Since I was the youngest, they decided to try to find a home for me. My grandparents knew of a newly married couple who were apparently having a difficult time conceiving a child of their own. With me in tow, my grandfather showed up at this couple's door and made his plea. He explained that they just could not care for me, and if the couple did not take me in then, they had no option except to turn me over to the state to raise.

What is so amazing to me is that, as I step back and look at the big picture, I see this young couple who were right smack-dab in the middle of their own pain. Before this couple married, they had discussed their desire to have a large family. They had just found out the news that they were unable to have children of their own and were in a dark place. Now, in the midst of their brokenness, they were presented with the option to take this child or else. Whatever this couple decided at this exact moment in time was going to determine the fate of that child, me.

Lucky for me, God had a plan, you see. His plan was to give me hope and a future, remember? So, this couple said yes and we became a family. I cannot begin to tell you the impact this event has had on my life—not only on the opportunities that I would be given in life, but also from the standpoint of being rescued from my circumstances. It seemed that God has always taken care of me, even when I could not take care of myself.

If you knew me, you would know that I have a slightly rebellious spirit, lots of energy, and am curious as a cat. I want to experience all life has to offer and leave no stone unturned. I do not like to cross the line, but I like to walk right up to it and look over. If I had remained in my birth family or had been a child of the state, I doubt very seriously that I would be alive today to tell this story. I have never done drugs; I detest cigarettes and alcohol. However, I promise you, if I had not been given this chance in life, I would have fallen prey to all of them. My life would have been a disaster. I know myself well enough to know that I would have tried and done anything to fulfill the drive and need that I have in my soul to have fun, seek a thrill, and find love.

Thank goodness I was given two loving parents who taught me right from wrong. They took me to church and gave me a solid foundation. They protected me and pulled back on my leash when I needed it. I am so grateful that my mother knew me better than I knew myself. She said no at times when I wanted to go somewhere or do something.

It made me so angry at the time, but now I see she knew exactly what she was doing. She was protecting me from myself. I can promise you that was not an easy task. To say "thank you, Mom" doesn't begin to express my feelings.

My father loved me unconditionally and gave me so much more than the required food, clothing, and shelter. Dad gave me an outlook on life that has been my guiding light for all these years. I am one fortunate girl and eternally grateful for everything my parents have done for me.

He who provides for this life, but takes no care for eternity, is wise for a moment, but a fool forever. -John Tillotson

෫ My Salvation ෭

After my adoption, the next big life-altering event that took place in my life happened at age sixteen. I was always a good kid growing up. I had a pleasing type of personality. I never wanted to disappoint my parents, so I pretty much obeyed the rules laid out for me, with the exception of meeting my curfew, which was always a problem for some reason. I was not really interested in getting into trouble, and I attended church and Sunday school. I had a great group of friends who were good influences in my life.

One day, a friend of mine asked me if I wanted to go to a revival with her at her church. I agreed, and not to my Lord's surprise, I would become a different person. J. Harold Smith was the pastor leading the message on that day. The scene was one typical of a Southern Baptist revival. There was some shouting and spitting, and his message was about knowing the outcome on the day we die. Did we know for sure where we would spend eternity? Pretty direct sermon, wouldn't you say? To be honest, it was a scary sermon. He really scared the bejeebies out of me. Let me say I know from growing up in the South that many sermons were fear-based, because in the Baptist church, you have two choices: heaven or hell. Some preachers realized a good way to get you to heaven was to literally scare the hell out of you! At any rate, I was not absolutely sure where I would go after I died. If being a good person could get me in through the pearly gates, then I had a fighting chance. But if it took anything else, I was in trouble.

According to this pastor, all I had to do was repent of my sins and ask Jesus to come into my heart, and that would begin my relationship with Jesus and guarantee me a spot in heaven. Hey, I was all for it! I went down to the altar that night and I prayed and asked Jesus to come into my heart. What was really surprising about all of this is that, when I made that decision to ask Jesus to come in and dwell inside of me, He didn't just quietly come in unnoticed. Jesus exploded into my soul. I have never been able to deny the realness of that moment. From that day forward, I have never felt the absence of His presence in my heart. Jesus did indeed take up residence in my life. Here I am, almost three decades later, and I have never been without His sweet presence in my life. I may have been scared into a conversion, but I have been loved into a long-term affair with a loving God. It is the single most precious gift of my life. My time on Earth has been worth it all, just because I have had all the years to bond with a God that is in love with me!

It wasn't long after my conversion that I got baptized. When I walked down the aisle at my home church to let the congregation know of my conversion, much to my surprise, my dad was right behind me. Is God's planning perfect or what?

My dad has always embraced the Presbyterian belief that states moderation in all things. He is gentle and kind and gets along with everyone. I am not sure what decision he made that morning. All I know is, he walked down the aisle and he attended church more frequently with us on Sundays instead of playing golf.

On the day of my baptism, I can remember hearing the words of my pastor saying, "We are buried with Christ in baptism and resurrected to walk in newness of life," and as I was walking out of the baptismal pool, I looked back at the water. I actually felt as if I had deposited the old life in the tank, and I wondered if the water was murky. I felt clean and literally *reborn.*

My spiritual journey since that time has taken me down many roads. I am still growing and learning. I have some unanswered questions that remain difficult for me at times to just accept and move on. However, I have come to a place in life where I do not have to have all the answers in order to believe. I think that is why they call it faith.

For me, there has been a constant presence of the spirit I asked into my heart when I was sixteen years old. I cannot deny that. I find joy in worshipping a God whom I believe created all that is. I find peace in believing there is a home waiting for me after this life is over, and that my loved ones will be there as well. Do I know that this is how things are going to happen? No. But do I choose to believe that? Yes, for some reason, I cannot help but believe. I get to worship with a body of believers who are good people. I have peace and joy in my life. I have a book of guidelines that encourages me to treat my fellow humans with a servant's heart, and what could be more important in this life than to be a good human?

There is more room in Christ, in God, in heaven to give me rest and peace and joy than in the whole universe to disquiet trouble and grieve me. —author unknown

Life is to be enjoyed, not simply endured. Pleasure and goodness and joy support the pursuit of survival. -Willard Gaylin

ೞ **Divorce** ೪

I wish I could skip this section of my life. It is the darkest and most disappointing part. I have always felt like a winner and an overcomer. The divorce, however, marked my first big failure, and it felt like I had a black mark in my life.

Like so many girls do, I got married because I was ready to get married and start playing house. I had graduated from college, had a fun job as a flight attendant, and was living with two girls in an apartment in Atlanta. Everything was coasting along in fine fashion. I have always had ants in my pants, and once I accomplish something, it is on to the next thing for me. It isn't a trait I am particularly proud of, but it is what it is. So having achieved all the goals I had set, it was time to move on to the next natural stage of my life: marriage. Without any prospects, I did what I do best. I set myself a goal and began working to achieve that goal. Keep in mind, I was about twenty-two years of age when I started this quest.

People all over the world marry for all sorts of reasons. Some Mr. Rights end up being Mr. Right Now. Some marry for security, others because they are lonely and a warm body beats no body. I married because I was ready to move on to the next chapter of my life, and I honestly thought if I married a good Christian man, then we could work through any difficulty and would never divorce. I married that good Christian man, and he was also a great dad, good provider, and overall good person.

We ended up being a great team. We served in the community and in our church. We led small groups and for thirteen years we rarely had an argument. With all of this going on, one might wonder how in the world things could go so wrong. The problem was, I got the cart before the horse. I got ahead of God. I told God this was what I was going to do and hoped He would bless us. I found out the hard way that God does not work that way. We would always be a team, but I knew there was something more that I was missing.

We started reading marriage books, and I learned all about love languages and love tanks that needed to be filled. I learned how to fight fair and the importance of having a date night. But all the rules of engagement and all the wishful thinking were not going to make us work. We did not have a bond between us that made us want to curl up on the couch together. The longer we stayed married, the more our differences became a point of contention.

I know that there are marriages all over the world made up of opposites, yet somehow they work. I think they must have something else that keeps them together, something we just did not have. I honestly believed that our years together were going to be spent surviving and not really living. So I made the decision to end it after thirteen years instead of thirty, and I believe we are *both* happier now because of it.

It seems strange to me how one couple can meet and marry within a couple of weeks before he heads off to war, and they live happily ever after. Then you have another couple who meet in high school and date through college and then marry after a long courting process, only to despise each other a few years later.

I know all marriages take work, but with half of our marriages ending in divorce, I am now trying to figure out how I can serve the people who have gone through the same traumatic event.

Those of us who have not been blessed to find our "one true north" on the first try are just as disappointed in ourselves as some of the first-timers may be in us. So what I am asking for here is a little mercy.

Should two people stay in a situation where "happily ever after" is more like "happy if I could just get out"? And should people be ostracized or looked down upon for making changes in their lives in order to find peace and joy? I felt so helpless when I got divorced. I could not stay and pretend everything was fine, and I could not make things better. If I could have, I would have snapped my fingers and made things all better and kept my family unit intact, as I believe most people would. But for me, love just doesn't work that way.

The one good thing to come out of this period of my life is that for the first time, I felt like I really needed God. My life had been so easy up until this point; though I had a love for God, I did not really have a need for Him. But now, I was desperate for Him and He was there. When everyone else hit the door, He was there with arms open wide. That is the God I serve, the God that says, "I will never leave you or forsake you."

If you ask me my opinion on divorce today, these are my thoughts. I learned in counseling that if you started your marriage off with God joining the two of you together and there was a great love there, then God can put it back together should you ever get into trouble. It takes an enormous amount of work from both parties, but it can be done!

On the other hand, if your Mr. Right just happened to be Mr. Right Now, or if you were young and you made a mistake, or you jumped ahead of God's plan for your life like me, it is sometimes difficult to fix. So many women in my parents' generation chose to stick it out and live unhappily ever after. For me, life is too short to get to the end of it only to find it was a life endured, not fully lived.

My ex also seems to be more alive and in love than I have ever seen him. He has found the gal who rocks his world and I am so happy for them both.

If you are in a bad marriage right now, I suggest you get counseling before you make any decision to divorce. It will teach you so much about yourself and your spouse. Plus it will better equip you to make a better choice next time, should it not save your current marriage.

I would also suggest that you not beat yourself to a bloody pulp over your split. Trust me, God is bigger than our failures, and He will love you no matter what.

Peace is the quiet place under the mighty wing of God.

Life shrinks or expands in proportion to one's courage.

⊂з Knowing Thyself &ᴑ

I think it is very important to know and love yourself. I spent three years really getting to know myself. I wanted a fuller knowledge of who I really was. That was the easy part. The hard part came in finding a way to love that person. The truth of the matter is, God created you and me just the way we are. It is up to us to live the best life possible, using the personality God gave us. For instance, God created me with this energetic, restless, independent, slightly reckless nature. All of these qualities can be used for good or for bad, and it is up to me to channel these in a way that will be pleasing to the Father. I will be the first to admit that I have not always succeeded. Every day it seems like a battle.

With this personality, I have choices to make. I know God can use me to love the people in my world. In order for Him to do that, though, I must harness the qualities that are in conflict with His mission for me. In order to do that, I must identify those qualities and learn how they can cause pain to others as well as myself. For instance, I am quick at everything,thus I tend to get slightly frustrated with people who aren't. Just because I can fly through my tasks does not mean I need to jump on those I love because they are not just like me.

Knowing who I am has helped me make adjustments in my personal life. If I know that I must have certain things occur in a day to feel good, then I am going to make sure those things are a priority. That is not to say that the goal always gets accomplished, but I do have a good concept of what it takes for me to live a balanced, happy life. I try not to put many things above my "needs" list.

One of the most important things about knowing yourself is realizing that you never arrive. It is definitely a journey, not a destination. I am constantly assessing my life and asking myself if I need to change anything or if I am falling short in any area of my life. Do I need to improve my patience level? Am I playing too much and not tasking enough (a big problem with us recreation majors). If I let my life go without thinking about it, then I do not feel as if I am being the best *me* that I can be.

Another important thing to remember in knowing thyself is that not everyone is just like you, so cut them a break. I know I am an outdoor gal who does not really enjoying sitting in front of a television set. I must get in some sort of exercise every day. I do not like to sit around and "visit." I like animals and I am a free thinker. I try to see every person as a human first and not be distracted by the events of that person's life, whether good or bad. I detest drama and trauma, and I do not handle whiners very well. With all of that said, for me to expect other people to be just like me would be ludicrous. I love the diversity of people. I hold myself above no one. I am flesh and blood, with likes and dislikes. That is all. No more, no less. My accomplishments do not elevate me above anyone, and I am not better than anyone because I never did this or that, and I am no less than anyone because I did this or that. I am just me and you are just you. Why have we as a society not learned to embrace difference? We want everyone to believe just like we do. We want to be right at all costs. We are alienating more people than we love, and something is wrong with that, I believe.

I urge you to get to know the real you. Commit to liking that person. If there are things that need to be changed, then work on them. If there are areas of excess, cut back. If you need more friends, work at being a friend. You do not have to master all the areas; just work on them. It is a long road and it will take you awhile to get there, so do not get too frustrated that it may not all get done today. I am amazed that every day I seem to find out something new about myself. I will do or say something and wonder, "What in the heck is up with that?" or "Where did that come from?" It is important to understand why you are the way you are, and it is more important not to stop there. I have heard it said that the events in your life might explain why you do something, but it does not excuse you. At some point in life, you must take responsibility for your own actions.

It would pay to take a good look at your life and find out just what it is that you think defines you. Is it your job, your looks, your talents, your accomplishments? If you are depending on these externals, then you are walking on thin ice, my friend. You better like yourself from the inside out or you are setting yourself up for a fall. These things will let you down every time. A great example of this from my own life comes from going from first to worst on a reality show. Internally, it had zero impact on me emotionally. I believe that stems from not allowing a television show to define who I am. I am not "Tina the *Survivor* girl" but rather "Tina, lover of life"!

I believe we choose our own happiness. I believe we can find a way when it seems as if the road is a dead end. I do not think it is someone else's responsibility to make sure I am happy or to see to it that my best interest is looked after. No one can do that but me. I encourage you to take control of what you already possess: the ability to be happy.

If you have never been scared or embarrassed or hurt, it means you've never taken many chances. —Author unknown

Daily Devotionals

In order to make these devotionals a little different than your average ones, I actually took my journal and looked at the entries that I have written over the years. Then I rewrote them to be in a more devotional style. So what you are reading will be thoughts I was having at some point in time, and I am now sharing them with you.

My goal is to hopefully open myself up to you, the reader, but more so to encourage you to be a good human and to love your fellow man more deeply and gracefully.

Remember, this is not my time, but rather your time with God to sit and ponder and question. I am sure He loves having your undivided attention, if only for a little while.

I wish you great adventures in your life and to live the life less ordinary!

ೞ A GRATEFUL HEART ೲ

Colossians 2:6, 7

"So then, just as you received Christ Jesus as Lord, continue to live in him, rooted and built up in him, strengthened in the faith as you were taught, and overflowing with thankfulness."

"Overflowing with thankfulness" — what a concept! I am not sure when the feeling of thankfulness took up residence in my soul. It may have been in college, when I first began working with individuals who had physical challenges. It may have been after a time of lengthy counseling. It may have been a part of my being due to the situation surrounding my adoption. The exact time and place of its inception may be a mystery, but what I know for sure is that I am living with a grateful heart. I am so thankful and appreciative of all that God has given me.

Sometimes when I go for a walk, I feel so much appreciation for my two legs that work, for the air that I am able to breathe on my own, for the place in which I live, for where I am in life, and for the peace within my soul. I walk along and my heart feels so full that I think I may not be able to contain it all.

I feel this way a good portion of my waking hours. I am thankful for even the little things. It seems that as my day goes along, I may see things that remind me how much I have to be grateful for. If I see a hitchhiker, I am thankful for my car. If I pass an ambulance, I pray for the injured within and thank God for my safety. If I pass the rescue mission, I am thankful for the people in my life who love and care for me. When I pass drivers who look like they swallowed sour grapes, I thank God for the joy I have in my life. When I get home and my dog comes to greet me, I thank God for creating pets that love us so openly and unconditionally. How can one be in a bad mood when there is so much to be thankful for? I certainly can't.

I challenge you, as you go throughout your day, to list all the things that you have to be thankful for. Let the day's events remind you of all you have and all the wonderful blessings that you receive every single day.

Prayer: Father, thank you for the place I am in right now. It is good. Let me never forget what all you have done and continue to do for me. Help others see all the gifts you have given to them and to be mindful of them.

List the top ten things you are grateful for.

_____

_____

_____

_____

_____

_____

_____

_____

_____

☙ A TIME TO WEEP ❧

Ecclesiastes 3:1, 2, 4
"There is a time for everything and a season for every activity under heaven: a time to be born and a time to die, a time to weep and a time to laugh."

I got the news this week that person I grew up with committed suicide. My heart sank and I cannot seem to stop thinking about him. I think about the family that is left behind, and I wonder how anyone can be that sad. Why can't people find the strength to change their circumstances or find some relief for their sadness? I understand some people are chemically unbalanced, and yet I know they make medication to help with that. I understand that some may feel like there are no good answers for what they have to deal with, but death is not the best solution, because it is a permanent one.

I am such a fixer and evaluator. The moment a glimpse of unhappiness comes along, I am on it like a superhero wanting to fight evil and restore peace and harmony. I do most of my activities alone and most of them are outside, so I have plenty of time to self-evaluate and talk with God.

There was a time in my life when I was up against a battle that I was not sure I could win. I was sad for a while, and yet what sustained me was hope. I had great hope that God was going to do a miracle and change my situation. I did not just pray. I prayed with the belief that it *was* going to happen. Sometimes, when we are at our lowest moments, that is all we can do. Tomorrow is always another day with opportunities we know nothing of. Just hold on and wait and believe that help is on the way, and keep fighting. Do not give up. When you give up, that is when you lose hope, and without hope we die, leaving the masses sad and missing the one they lost.

Prayer:

Father, I wish no one felt so hopeless they thought life was not worth living. Today I ask for comfort for anyone who feels afraid, lonely, empty, scared, or sad. Please comfort and give them hope. Be with the families of all who have lost loved ones today. Let the sun peek through the clouds just for them.

When have you felt like you were at rock bottom and God lifted you up?

_____

_____

_____

_____

_____

_____

_____

_____

_____

‹ൠ AMAZING LOVE ൠ›

Psalms 33:5
"The Lord loves righteousness and justice; the earth is full of his unfailing love."

Do you ever have periods in your life when everything just seems perfect? Do you ever feel so complete and content that it is almost scary? It might be that you get a glimpse of how good God has been in your life and the joy just pours out of you. That is how I feel right now in my life.

I have two great kids, , and I am in good enough health (despite having arthritis) that I am able to enjoy the great outdoors almost every day. Who could ask for more? I feel so loved by my heavenly Father.

I wish for one moment I could tap into the love of God—a love so amazing that he rescued me from a life of hardship and put me into a family that would nurture me and grow me into what I am today. He did that just for me.

It is a love so amazing that He would give broken bodies like Mattie Stepanek's wings to soar above this Earth and bless everyone who reads his books of poetry. Muscular dystrophy limited his body from being an active participant on this Earth to some degree, but God's love came in and no one could stop this little lover from blessing the world through the words that flowed from his precious heart.

It is because of God's love that missionaries leave the comforts of home to share the love that flows through their veins. The sacrifices they make seem like token matters to them. They have to share God with the people of their world. It matters not to them what it costs.

What God pours into each of us just cannot be kept to ourselves. We want to share this gift. It pours out of each of us. It is a love so divine, I hardly can contain its fullness in my soul. Today I am mindful of how much my Father loves me. He died for me and now I live for him. I want to live so fully alive that there is no doubt to anyone that He dwells in my soul.

Prayer:

Father, your love is filling me today. There are no holes, no missing pieces; nothing feels broken. I am complete and happy, and feel so loved by you. This harmony and peace is a gift that can only come from you. My hope is that you will feel loved by me.

What are you doing to spread God's love?

_____

_____

_____

_____

_____

_____

_____

_____

og AMAZING WOMEN so

Matthew 25:21
"His master replied, 'Well done, good and faithful servant!
You have been faithful with a few things; I will put you
in charge of many things. Come and share your master's
happiness.'"

One of my favorite movies is *Steel Magnolias*. It is a movie about strong women of the South. Do not get me wrong; I do not think that we Southern belles have a corner on the market. I think women are an amazing breed of humans. It seems that God must have known that our role would be an important one in society and so He created us equipped to fulfill that role.

There are a few women out there who make me want to put on my Helen Reddy CD and shout "I am woman, hear me roar!" One such woman is Oprah Winfrey. She is such an icon that it looks funny putting her last name on this page. We all know her just as Oprah. I cannot imagine accomplishing in my lifetime everything that this woman has been able to do in her short time here on Earth.

What impresses me so much about this special soul is that she did not have a foot in the door or know somebody; nor was she born into a life of privilege. All of these things would have given her a foothold with which to propel herself and her work here on Earth to a higher level. Her foothold was instead life experiences and her drive. She had a belief that she could make a difference in the world.

I am sure when Oprah was twelve and thirteen years old, she was not thinking, "One day I am going to be a movement and one of the most powerful women in the world." But what *was* happening was that God was looking down and saw this girl who had something special about her. I think it may be like what God saw when looking down on His servant Job. God was so impressed and pleased and proud of His servant. I think He sees the same thing in Oprah. He gave her the gift to be different. I think it has been an amazing collaboration. Oprah has held up her end of the stick and God has done His part to open doors for her to step through and make amazing things happen. I think, if we were to know all the people who have been touched by this one woman, we would be amazed. She is a movement. She is a light. But to be honest, she is us.

If we wanted to, we all could get on the bus of "being the change we wish to see in the world"(Gandhi). I believe the world is ours to love, to minister to, to change for the better. Oprah just happens to believe it with such a faith that she cannot be stopped! Well done, good and faithful servant.

Prayer:

Lord, I pray for an Oprah movement in us all. Help us, God, to believe that we can make a difference in the world. Even if we may not go global like Oprah, we can move in our towns, our neighborhoods, and even in our families.

What could you do to be a movement in your neighborhood, work, or school?

_____

_____

_____

_____

_____

_____

_____

_____

_____

❧ BALANCE ❧

Daniel 12:3
"Those who are wise will shine like the brightness of the heaven…"

Balance: this one little word may be the most important word in the quest for being happy in your everyday life. It is a word that I think about daily. When I must make a choice, I think about it. When I plan my day and week, I think about it. When I get a phone call and am asked to do something, I think about it.

I want to be a productive person and do as much as I can for others, but I must remember to include myself in that list. If I have plans for myself on a given day, then I try and keep that date with myself.

There are a few things that I know I have to do in every given day to feel balanced. For instance, I know I need to exercise. Sometimes that has meant getting up earlier than I normally would in order to get that need in. I have to fight the urge to fill that time with something "more important" like sleep.

House chores are the worst! There are things that have to be done, and this is where I really have to be disciplined. I hate housecleaning. I have to make myself stay home and pick up and do laundry or any other number of things that scream at me for attention. If I am balanced and have kept to my routine, then I have had enough playtime and Tina time that I do not resent the time I have to spend doing chores.

I have learned how to balance my life, and I am completely content with the arrangement that I have with myself. My life seems calm and I have learned how to say, "No, I am sorry I can't fit that in this week" and not feel a bit bad about it.

Being balanced also makes you a pleasant person to be around. I know what it feels like to have everyone tugging at me when I haven't had a moment to myself. It is quite ugly and I do not recommend it. How many times have I snapped at my kids because I have not been a good manager of my time?

I want to encourage you to sit down today and make out a perfect-day list for yourself. Try to keep it as realistic as possible. I know we would all like to start out our day with a body massage, but that isn't really feasible, is it? So what is it that you need every day to make it a good day?

I have been blessed beyond my wildest dreams. I do not have to work a forty-hour work week, and for that I am grateful. I have, however, walked in those shoes as well. For those of you who work full time and are managing a family, it is not so easy, and living a balanced life takes a little more planning and effort. You have to choose what is *most* important. For instance, I know that I am going to be most happy if I can fit exercise into my day somewhere. When I was working full time, it meant that I had to get up at five thirty in the morning in order to get to the gym before work. To me, my exercise was such a high priority that I was willing to make that sacrifice. Each of us has things in our lives that we need. The question is, what are you willing to do to make sure that those needs are met? At times it may mean that you do not meet the needs of someone else in order to take care of yourself. Is that selfish? Absolutely not. Give yourself permission to do what it takes to be a healthy you.

It may be that you order pizza and invite your neighbor over instead of cooking a home-cooked meal. It may mean you ask your husband to pull the load of clothes out of the washer and put it in the dryer for you. (It won't kill him.) It is amazing what an extra couple of hours of sleep will do for your body. Give yourself permission to go to bed early one night.

Get creative. Be a good time manager. But whatever you do, spend some time thinking about balance and apply it to your life. You will be doing yourself and everyone else in your life a big favor.

Prayer:

Lord, help us to be at peace with ourselves. We women are such worker bees, feeling responsible for everybody, it seems. Help us to work at being balanced and show us where we are out of kilter, and may you always take precedence in our lives, putting you first on our list.

Is your life balanced? What would you be willing to give up in order to have more time for yourself?

_____

_____

_____

_____

_____

_____

_____

_____

_____

_____

❧ BE A GOOD HUMAN ❧

John 13:14-17
"'Do you understand what I have done for you?' he asked
them. 'You call me Teacher and Lord, and rightly so, for
that is what I am. Now that I your Lord and Teacher have
washed our feet, you also should wash one another's feet. I
have set you an example that you should do as I have done
for you. I tell you the truth, no servant is greater than his
master, nor is a messenger greater than the one who sent
him. Now that you know these things, you will be blessed
if you do them.'"

Dale and I recently went camping and we took a bike ride off the beaten path. We came upon an old cemetery and we looked at some of the tombstones. Some of them even had photos of the deceased attached to them. Dale made the comment, "These people worked from daylight to dark, and all for what? There probably isn't a person alive today that remembers they even lived. They all just lived and died." In thinking about that, I realized how most all of us are in that same situation. Unless we create some life-changing invention, find the cure for cancer, or have some outstanding talent, in a couple of generations, we will be a forgotten memory. With that in mind, I honestly believe that the most important time we have is the here and now—not our tomorrows or our yesterdays. And the most important thing we can do here and now is to be a good human to the people of our world right now while we are alive. We are just passing through, and I for one do not want to get to the end of my life and ask, "What was it all for?" 1Timothy 6:7-8 says, "For we brought nothing into this world, and we take nothing out of it. But if we have food and clothing, we will be content with that."

I personally feel it is not about us, me, and I. It is about what we do for others and the kindness we extend. Being a good human entails much more than being a morally good person. It is about the little things like opening doors, letting cars go in front of us, listening more than we talk, asking people questions about themselves, being generous to those in need, not acquiring things for ourselves, but instead traveling and experiencing the beauty of this world we temporarily call home. We can enjoy serving and not feeling like someone must serve us. Compliment people because it makes them feel good, and say "please" and "thank you," not just because it is good manners but because you mean it. If someone is in an awkward situation, try to help without drawing attention to it or making a big deal about it. See those less fortunate as just that, not as underachievers or lazy or less than yourself. When making eye contact when walking in malls or airports, initiate saying hello or at least smile at the person you meet eyes with. Why wait for them? Be really radical and wave at strangers. Tell people they are pretty. Everybody could use a compliment.

One of my favorite things to do is touch. When I talk to people, I like to touch their hand or shoulder from time to time, because human contact is a good thing. I like to hug instead of shake hands.

I do not keep a lot of extra stuff around the house. I do not see the need to have fifty washcloths. If I have extra of anything, I try to find someone to give the excess to. All that "free" shampoo, lotion, and cream rinse at hotels: Give them to the women's shelter. There are so many things you can do to give to other people. You can send thank-you notes, invite people to do things, offer to drive, offer to pay, give little gifts, or just give a card or make a phone call. Show the people you love how important they are and let them know how special they are to you. Tell the people of your world exactly what it is you like about them.

When I check out of this life, I want to go out knowing I gave myself to others and that I loved to the best of my ability. Moms and dads, start teaching this to your children now. Show them by example. Do random acts of kindness like paying for the meal behind you at the pickup window at McDonald's. Put your children in situations where they are the givers. The world opposes this concept, and it is up to you to fight the "it is all about me" mentality our society embraces.

I would like to challenge you for one full day to be totally selfless. Start the day with doing something nice for your spouse if you are married. Bring him or her a cup of coffee and deliver it with a kiss or an "I love you" attached. If you are single, go to your window and look outside for two or three minutes at the beauty of your world. Is the sun shining? Is the rain pouring down to water the trees that shade you? Maybe there is even snow that brought hours of fun making snowballs or sledding in your youth. Take a minute to wonder in it.

While you get ready, think about how lucky you are to have that closet full of clothes. Are you blessed to have a good job? When is the last time you let your boss know you appreciate the opportunity to work for him? Do you have good eyesight and limbs that work? You could use them to help any of the multiple organizations that assist people who are not as fortunate. Do you have people in your life who love you? Tell them you appreciate them. Is there food in your pantry? Are your clothes clean? Did you get a warm shower this morning? On and on this list goes. I have traveled this world enough to know that I have so much to be thankful for, and to be just a taker would be shameful.

For the next few hours, give, give, and give. See how much you can give just for fun for one day. Be conscious of it. Watch people's response to you. Hear the tone in their voices when they say thank you. Then, at the end of the day, think about how little it cost you. Make it a habit. I think liking yourself is important, and living by giving will only enhance your self-worth.

Let me give you an example of a life self-focused. Just the other day, I was at an NFL football game. Sitting behind me was a man who was becoming quite distressed about a row of people sitting in front of me. These folks kept getting up and going to the snack bar, restroom, and who knows where else. Luckily there was a huge Jumbotron screen at both ends of the field. So for those few plays that we missed, we could catch them on the screens and see the play directly. Thank goodness for Jumbotron, right? Wrong!

The man behind me was so angry. He was screaming at these folks and getting all worked up. Never mind that it was a glorious night or that he was fortunate enough to have tickets to the game. I am sure he was not thinking about how blessed he was to be in such good health that he was physically able to make the trek to the game and to his seat. All this man saw was that his primary view was temporarily obstructed. You know what I find funny about this? It was a preseason game, and the game was not even close! It amazes me that people lose sight of what is important and what is not. Like Richard Carlson said, "Don't sweat the small stuff, and remember, everything is small stuff."

Being a good human starts and ends with you. That is one thing you can control in life. It may not make people remember your name in a hundred years, but it has the potential to brighten the world of countless people you come into contact with every single day.

Prayer:

Lord, show us how to live. Teach us to live lives that are good and giving. We do not wash each other's feet anymore, but we can still do so much to serve the people in our world. You did it and told us to live by your example. Help us to see how we can do that on a daily basis.

List some ways you would like to be a good human today.

_____

_____

_____

_____

_____

_____

_____

_____

_____

ᙍ CELEBRATION ᔑ

Luke 15:6
"Then he calls his friends and neighbors together and says 'Rejoice with me: I have found my lost sheep.' I tell you that in the same way there is more rejoicing in heaven over one sinner who repents than over ninety-nine righteous persons who do not need to repent."

And the angels rejoiced, though I am sure they are not whooping and hollering half as much as I am. You see, a dear friend of mine who was an unbeliever has just become blinded by the light. I have two friends who are hardcore cynics. One did not really have a problem with God, but it was the three-in-one thing and Jesus dying and coming back to life that was just too much to grasp. The other friend believes God is birthed out of human necessity. He thinks we humans must have the comfort we seek by creating someone bigger, better, and stronger than ourselves and placing Him in control. He thinks we need comfort in thinking there is an afterlife, so we can find a meaning and purpose in living and dying.

I have been a friend of both of my doubting Thomases for quite some time. I am not known for my shyness, so I have talked to both until I was blue in the face. I have prayed (in all earnest) and even begged for mercy from the highest court for the souls of my two friends. Finally, I resigned myself to "Lord, if it is going to happen, it will have to be from You, because I have exhausted all my efforts." I left my friends in His able care (like mine was so much better). Do not get me wrong; I still take every opportunity to put in a good word in here and there about how great life is with my friend Jesus. I just cannot help myself.

Here is where the rejoicing comes in. Last week, I received a phone call from one of those dear souls. It seems that God had faithfully rescued one of my buddies. One would think that, after serving and watching the God of surprises for twenty-seven years, one would not be shocked anymore. But I must admit before the adulation was shock and amazement. Was it true?! How did it happen? Are you sure? Oh, praise God and thank you, Father! And, oh my friend, what a ride awaits you. I am still thanking God and rejoicing.

So now I have one down and one to go. But now my hope is even stronger. Maybe I should have placed them both in His able care to begin with.

Prayer:
Thank you, God, for pursuing us and loving us so much that you never give up hope on us. I am thankful beyond words for Your patience and Your love. Thank you for reminding me you are not working on a timetable.

Have you given up hope on a friend or loved one? Remember it is never too late. Write a prayer to God reminding Him that the lost still matter to you.

_____

_____

_____

_____

_____

_____

_____

_____

☙ **CHANGE** ☙

Matthew 18:3
"I tell you the truth, unless you change and become like little children, you will never enter the kingdom of heaven."

Some people hate change. They find it disturbing and fearful. Not me! I welcome change and even search it out. It used to be that, when I was working a steady job, I would drive a different way to work from time to time, just for a change of scenery. I like to change the furniture arrangement in the house. I change my exercise routine. I change my voice mail recording. I love the change of seasons (with the exception of winter). For me the only good thing about winter is that it makes you appreciate spring.

Right now, fall is in the air. All of nature is changing before me. The hot, humid days have become cool and brisk. The leaves are turning from green to reds and yellows. I have changed out the flowers in my flowerbeds. Mums are now welcoming my visitors, instead of impatiens.

Change is a good thing. I enjoy looking inside of me and asking myself, "Do I need to change anything?" That could mean a thought, a feeling, a point of view, or a habit.

Change for me means not getting what you've always gotten. It means seeing with new eyes. It means every day is new day with limitless opportunities. I never want to get stuck. Is there anything you need to change today?

Prayer:

Lord, let me always be open-minded enough to see where I need work. Thank you for all the opportunities you give me to see things differently. Lord, may even my love for you continue to change and grow year after year, through every season of my life.

What in your life is in need of a change?

_____

_____

_____

_____

_____

_____

_____

_____

✂ COMMUNICATION ✂

1 Corinthians 13:4-5
"Love is patient, love is kind. It does not envy, it does not boast, it is not proud. It is not rude, it is not self-seeking, it is not easily angered, it keeps no record of wrongs."

What can I possibly say about communication that has not been said before? We all know of the importance of having it in any relationship. The longer I live the more I experience the different ways in which people communicate. There are those who are non-confrontational and would rather sacrifice their own needs in order to just keep the peace. There are those who do not have a large degree of patience and bark their demands without regard to the other person's feelings. There are also people out there who clam up and communicate best by pouting.

An interesting observation of the people I communicate with is that some take responsibility for fault while others are sure it is always someone elses fault.

There was a time in my life when I was the clam. I pouted and used non-verbal skills to let the world know

I was unhappy. I guess I thought it was up to whomever to figure out just what it was that had me upset. I was a disaster area. The one gift that counseling and failure taught me, was to express my feelings and the proper way to do it. I now feel as if I want to talk about everything. I want to be in the know of everything. I ask my kids questions constantly. I also like to use the 1-10 scale. For example, I will ask my kids on a scale of 1-10 how well did you enjoy your vacation? That really helps me to know exactly where they are with things. I am sure that I drive them crazy, but there is something about being clamed up for so many years that now makes me want to talk and to share everything.

I also feel as if I can now communicate in a way that is not threatening to the person I am talking to, even if we are in conflict mode. I try to not let my emotions get involved and I try to concentrate on what the other person is feeling and how things look from their side of the fence. I want to express my side and my feelings, but I am doing so while considering them. This method has served me well. It cost me nothing to try to understand how the other person must feel. It makes me more understanding and hopefully easier to talk with. The more a couple communicates the better off any relationship is going to be.

When in communication with others I think if you can learn to get your point across without being critical of that person, you also gain a level of trust. My kids know that they can come talk to me about anything and even if I do not agree with what they are telling me, I am not going to criticize them. Against my wishes my daughter recently got a tiny stud nose piercing. Personally I have always found it takes away from ones appearance rather than adding to.

Now that is MY personal opinion. I realize someone else may have a different opinion. So, when she told me about it I expressed my opinion but never did I attack her. As a parent that is not easy to do. We want to try to remain in control of our children, even when they are grown.

The most important thing I have learned about communication is that it is the key to growth. If there is a clear, safe line of communication between couples then it is only going to serve to improve the relationship. If a parent has an open, and interested line available to their kids, then there is a good chance the bond is going to be closer between them. The key is learning to talk where the words are positive or at least not hurtful to the other person and keep a focus on trying to understand where the other person is coming from.

Our mouth is our heart's voice box. It verbalizes whatever it is feeling. It would be such a gift to others if we could filter out the bad and voice only the good that we feel for others. I think that is an age-old problem, though one I doubt I can conquer in my lifetime.

Prayer:

Lord, you gave us a mouth to communicate. Help us to choose daily to use it for edifying and loving one another. Give us the courage to say we are sorry if we need to. May we try to build up one another and not tear each other down.

Are you a good communicator? What could you do to improve on your skills?

_____

_____

_____

_____

_____

_____

_____

_____

_____

❧ COMPASSION OVERFLOWING ❧

Lamentations 3:22-23
"Because of the Lord's great love we are not consumed, for his compassions never fail."

One of the reasons I am so in love with my heavenly Father is because of His ruthless love for his creation. Story after story in the Bible tells of His compassion. They sound so simple in word form, but if you have ever been on the receiving end of that love, the words cease to be letters formed to make sentences. They become examples of what you, too, have felt and now know to be true.

An example of what I am talking about was when God created Adam. He made him to rule over the Earth. The plants and animals were his only companions. God looked down and saw that he was lonely because there was no other such species like him. God spoke and said, "It is not good for man to be alone." So God created woman. You see, God knows when we are lonely and He cares. Have you recently lost a loved one, or has it been ages since you have been on a date? Guess what? God knows about matters of the heart, and our feelings are significant to the God of the universe.

Then there is Job. Job was a man God loved and even called faithful. He had so much faith in him that He allowed Satan to mess with him, knowing he would not waver. (I personally hope God doesn't have that much faith in me, and I find this passage a little disturbing.) Anyway, Satan wreaked havoc on poor Job, taking his crops, animals, family, and lastly his health. The only thing Job had left was his life. Dear Job proved faithful, but his mind was full of questions. Wouldn't yours be as well? Ever been there? You were serving God faithfully yet the unthinkable happened: death, rape, abandonment. God loved Job so much that He answered his questions. Job and God had a verbal dialogue. I ask God questions all the time but do not really expect to hear Him verbally answer me. God may use people, prayer, or even the Word or circumstance to help me find the answer I need, but I have never heard His voice. But God spoke to Job verbally.

One of my favorite stories of God's compassion comes from the woman at the well. She had been caught in adultery, and as was the custom back then, she was moments away from being stoned. I imagine this was a woman who did not attend church or go to the synagogue very often. She probably did not serve on religious committees, yet my God is her God. He stepped into that situation and spoke only one sentence that was so powerful that every one of her accusers dropped their stones and walked away. Do you accuse others? Are you without sin? Put down your stone and pick up mercy. That is the love of my God speaking.

Then there was this dude named Peter. My heart is engaged with this man and his story. It feels personal, too, because Peter loved Jesus so much. Peter was strong and I am sure he felt like a warrior for Christ, and maybe even somewhat protective of his friend. Yet when push came to shove, it was Peter who denied even knowing the man Jesus. Have you ever had that sinking feeling and kept asking yourself, "What have I done?" The warrior becomes a child, the mighty weak; all the success and confidence tumbles effortlessly in a moment's time. All it took was an act, a word, or a deed and time seemed to stop, and you were left standing but not sure if the legs were going to hold out. Many times they do not and you drop to your knees in shame and disappointment. How many times have I been there? But Jesus knows the condition of the heart, you see. Yes, Peter denied his friend three times, but that did not mean that he did not love his master. Jesus knew that. So after his resurrection, Jesus found Peter (like He finds all of us time and time again) and three times He asked His friend, "Peter, do you love me? Do you *really* love me?" Each sin was covered with love, and I think Jesus knew Peter needed to say those words.

I do not know about you, but too many times, my actions do not mirror my feelings. When I fail, I can usually be found groveling at my Savior's feet and I am telling Him, "Yes, Lord, I do love you, though my actions were anything but loving." The truth of the matter is I think that Jesus knows that most of us want to do the right thing. We came into this world unable to live the perfect life, as He did. I believe He feels somewhat sorry for us. I think He knows the struggles of our human condition. He did create us, you know. So instead of throwing stones, Jesus throws His love, mercy, and grace upon us and covers us from head to toe until we come running back to His arms where we are safe, protected, and loved.

The next time you are tempted to pick up a rock, why not try to pick up mercy instead and see what happens. This is a unique concept, I know, but if we are going to try to model our daily lives after this great man, that means we must also love those who try but fall short. Who knows? Maybe someone will throw mercy at you someday when you deserve rocks.

Prayer: My God, I cannot help but serve you. You resonate in my being. Your sweet music is in my ears. Your breath is sweet as it blows upon my face. You have lit my path and brought light to the darkness. You have stood unwavering on my behalf in the high court. Your eyes were fixed upon me, your presence ever near. Alive and well, you shout from my heart's chamber. You have loved, you have blessed, and you have forgiven. How could I not serve you, Father?

How has God shown compassion toward you?

_____

_____

_____

_____

_____

_____

_____

_____

og CONTENTMENT Ծ

1 Timothy 6:6
"But Godliness with contentment is great gain."

Contentment in some form or fashion is what we are all chasing. It hides behind different things, such as the almighty dollar, success, or that one true love. But in the end, it is contentment that we really desire. In the last two years, I have caught myself saying, "I just cannot imagine being any happier." When I say or think that thought, it still amazes me. I have been known to be more of a restless individual, and so to find myself in this wonderful place is quite new to me.

If a person has this quality, it shines and radiates from them. There is a sense that the person is content. They do not seem to be in need. They are not running around chasing something or looking around the room at a party to see who is there. They are content to talk to you, and you are the focus of their attention. They give of their time because their personal needs have been met, so they have more of themselves to give. The contented person is at peace with the world. They do not feel the need to change all the people who do not see things the way they do. It is a wonderful gift and one I do not take for granted.

I realize that life is not always easy. I have not always felt this way. But at this point in my life, I seem to have found a way to live here on this planet without letting life control me. It has taken me forty-five years, but I truly feel there are attitudes you can embrace that can cause you to live in the world but not be part of it. I can honestly say I feel like a visitor here, just passing through. I do not belong here. I do not own it and it does not own me. What this attitude has done is minimize the seriousness of chasing the American dream. Instead, I have broken it down to little life secrets that somehow work together to make me feel like the luckiest, most blessed woman on the planet.

The truth is, we must all find our own way. My path has not always been easy, and there have been plenty of mistakes along the way. Hopefully, I learned something from those events that turned those mistakes into lessons. And now I can live free from things that used to bind me and hold me captive.

If you asked me how to get to this wonderland place, I am not sure I could tell you specifically all you have to do. I do know that some of the ingredients include living a grace-filled life, knowing who you are deep within your being (get counseling if you want the truth to that question), finding true love or finding peace in your singleness, treating your body well, living the life you imagined, and learning that serving means more than being served. All these things will give you a good start, and then ask God to help you find the rest of the road to your own personal, contented place.

Prayer:

Lord, thank you for this time on the mountaintop. I know things can change so quickly, and I am not sure if I will be able to stay in this wonderful place of being. Thank you for showing me how to live and for allowing me so many wonderful privileges in life. I praise you.

What gets in the way of your contentment?

_____

_____

_____

_____

_____

_____

_____

_____

⬿ DADS ⬾

Psalms 103:13
"As a father has compassion for his children, so the Lord has compassion on those who fear him."

Many girls like myself grow up to be daddies' girls. That is a little strange, since most of the time, it is the mom who stays home with us and teaches all about girl things and boys and everything in between. But for some reason, our dads invade our hearts and there is a special place there that only they can fill.

My dad is not a large man physically, but his heart is bigger than the heart of anyone I have ever met. His gentleness is his greatest strength. With this amazing quality, he can somehow relate to everyone he meets and can transport himself into other people's shoes with ease. I've never heard my dad make an ugly comment about anyone or make a degrading slur about any ethnic group.

When it came to giving people second chances, my dad was the best. Jim McClain always thought that people could change and deserved a chance to prove it. Maybe that is why he would hire people out of prison and detox to work at his garden center.

My love for my dad started when I was just a little girl. I can remember not wanting to abide by my mom's rules, which meant wearing a dress to school at least two days a week. It was my dad who secretly suggested the plan of wearing shorts under my dress and then changing on the bus. It was also my dad who took me and got my waist-long hair cut above my ears so I could keep my hair out of my eyes while swimming on the swim team. (I thought my mom was going to kill him for that one.)

One of my fondest memories is of my dad teaching me to fish. His patience with me as a child was unending. He raised me to bait my own hook and to take my own fish off the line. We would go morning fishing and night fishing, and he even taught me how to fly fish. I cannot remember a single time that he got frustrated when I got my lure hung up or my line tangled for the umpteenth time.

My dad taught me to water ski and play tennis, and he never took it easy on me when we were competing against each other. When I finally beat him at something that was a day to truly celebrate. He made as big a deal out of it as I did.

The biggest gift my dad gave me,was loving me just as I was. He knew I was a tomboy; he celebrated that. I never had to be more or better or different for him to love me. I was perfect the way I was, at least in his eyes. This gift has endeared him to me forever, and that is why I will always be Daddy's little girl.

I do not think that we can tell our parents enough how much they mean to us. Take time today to tell your dad *thank you* for all things he has done for you and for how special he is.

Prayer:
Father, thank you for our dads and for everything they teach us. Thank you for all the sacrifices our dads make in order to provide for the family. Bless our dads and open our eyes to all they do.

What special qualities does your dad have that you would like to mirror?

_____

_____

_____

_____

_____

_____

_____

_____

⌘ DEAR DAVID ⌘

1 Samuel 13:14
"…the LORD has sought out a man after his own heart and appointed him leader of his people…"

Dear David, I wanted to write you a letter because I have been studying about you. I have so many questions to ask. You received the highest compliment from God when He said you were a man after his own heart. Wow! Now that is special. If I were to say that about someone, I would really have to think highly of that person. I would love for God to say that about me. I find it interesting that God would say that about someone like you. I do not mean to sound ugly when I say that, but I am sure you know what I mean. I do not think that I need to remind you that you did commit adultery and murder. To be honest, it gives me hope. And isn't it just like God to choose someone with faults and shortcomings to show us that it is not the perfect, shiny people who win his favor all the time. Your story gives all of humanity hope.

God says He looks at the heart. God looked into your heart and saw something more than sin. He saw a man who loved him, despite his actions. I think God knows we are made of flesh and blood and that there is but one perfect being that has ever walked this earth. I think God is very sympathetic to our humanness. He can somehow look past our flaws and see right into our heart.

David, I feel like you must have felt at times on your journey. I stumble and fall and think, how in the world could a holy God love someone like me? Did you ever feel that way? Did you ever wonder why in the world God continued to love you so much? It is an amazing love, isn't it? I know you know exactly what I am talking about: that sweet, unconditional love that breathes His Holy Spirit into us, giving us life!

The truth of the matter is you had some *great* qualities. You were so brave in fighting that giant. I think it was your faith, not your bravery, that impressed both God and me. You were also such a good king.

David, I just want you to know that I thank you for being real, warts and all. Had you been perfect and flawless, I do not think I would be as impressed with your story. By being you and being less than perfect, it opens the door for me to say, "God, we are all Davids in our weaknesses, but God, I want to be a David in my strengths as well!"

I cannot wait to meet you and talk with you more someday. We can swap stories of how God was faithful in our lives, and maybe sing one of your praise songs together. Hopefully I will get a new heavenly voice when I arrive; otherwise the singing offer is out!

Love,
Tina

Prayer:

Father, I want to thank you for including the story of David in the Bible. Thank you for showing me it was not the Pharisees that you loved the most. It was the Davids, with their imperfections and their failures. You are a great God to remind us of that!

How does it make you feel knowing of God's great love for a less-than-perfect man like David?

❧ EASTER STORY ❧

Luke 24:34
"There they found the Eleven and those with them, assembled together and saying, 'it is true! The Lord has risen and has appeared to Simon.'"

Having just celebrated the fact that our Lord did indeed arise, I am full of emotion. It is very easy for me to identify with all of the people in the Easter story.

I can walk in the shoes of Peter, who hid in shame, having denied his Savior, his Lord, his very best friend. Then the news came that Jesus was missing from the tomb. I wonder, did it cross Peter's mind that Jesus just might have been alive, and if He was alive, would He confront Peter on denying Him three times? Would Jesus have been angry? I am sure Peter was feeling ashamed and thinking, "How can I face Him?" Haven't we all been there: ashamed and unable to be in the presence of our Father, much less look Him in the eye?

Next in line is Mary Magdalene. She was there by the empty tomb in a state of confusion and severe grief. Unable to think clearly, she was trying to figure out where the body of Jesus was. Did someone take Him? Where was He? Who could do such a thing? In this state of confusion, I do not think the possibility of resurrection even entered her mind. I do not think she had moved past the initial grief of His death. She must have been in a fog. Then He appeared to her. Or did He? In her confused state, did she start to question her sanity and what she really saw? I mean, why oh why would

He reveal himself first to her, a woman? Could He really have loved her that much? It was not like she was holy like Mother Mary. Her life had been somewhat sordid in nature. If it were me, I would appear to my mother first, or maybe the disciples—certainly not to someone like her. Unworthiness: the plague of many of us Christians. I can most definitely relate.

Now I am each of the disciples. Each had walked with Him and saw all the miracles. It was an amazing time, but to rise from the dead? I can imagine them sitting there, still talking about their friend, and then all of a sudden, He appears! Truth! Validity! He truly is who He said He was. They had hoped He was the Messiah, but we are talking history here! They were part of a historic moment in time that was going to change the world. Have you ever doubted or had second thoughts?

I can relate to this myself. I am a woman living more than two thousand years after this event occurred. Yet I feel the emotions and weep for a man whom I never personally met in a physical way. I cry for His mother and for His followers. I am a woman who needed that tomb to be empty. I am a woman who realizes that my only hope lies in the fact that there is no body still lying in that tomb.

Today I am celebrating that He is who he said He was: the Savior of the world. And He is risen indeed!

Prayer:
Lord, today we celebrate your resurrection. Thank you for dying for us, then rising again. Thank you for being such a loving Savior, and I hope you feel loved and celebrated today.

Who do you most identify with in the Easter story?

_____

_____

_____

_____

_____

_____

_____

_____

_____

❦ EQUAL ❧

James 2:2-3

"Suppose a man comes into your meeting wearing a gold ring and fine clothes, and a poor man in shabby clothes also comes in. If you show special attention to the man wearing fine clothes and say, 'Here is a good seat for you,' but say to the poor man, 'You stand there or sit on the floor by my feet,' have you not discriminated among yourselves and become judges with evil thoughts?"

Upon reading this scripture verse today, I was reminded that we are all equal and to not single out anyone. It is one of those verses that reminds me how modern the scriptures can be. It also reminds me that, even back thousands of years ago, treating people with respect was of utmost importance.

A pet peeve of mine has long been seeing one person put him- or herself above someone else. As a matter of fact, I will go out of my way to speak to the less attractive, less popular, less wealthy, and sometimes less clean, and initiate conversation with these people first. How wonderful it is to feel like a somebody. I have been humbled on a couple of occasions to find out people I thought were ordinary were anything but. Thank goodness I did not write them off as someone below my standards. I would have been quite embarrassed.

We can carry this same thought over to ethnic equality. The truth is, it does not matter if a person's skin color is black, purple, or blue. We are flesh and blood, and as human as the next person. Who do any of us think we are, treating anyone lower than ourselves? I get hot just writing about it. There may be some differences in genetics and in social dynamics within our groups, but we are one race and that race is human. I am not so naive as to believe that we are all the same—period. But what I am saying is that we all have feelings, and we all basically have the same needs as far as food, clothing, and shelter goes. And I think we all want to love and be loved. That makes us all generally the same.

I challenge you today to take time to get to know those you think you would not have anything in common with. Strike up a conversation in the elevator today with someone different from yourself. Say hi to the outcast at your school. You just may be surprised at how much like you they really are.

Prayer:
Lord, may I see all people as equals. Let me blur the boundaries of money, power, and looks. We are all one people with hearts. This is all I need to know.

Do you have a difficult time accepting people different from yourself?

_____

_____

_____

_____

_____

_____

_____

_____

☙ FAITH ❧

Job 38:4
"Where were you when I laid the earth's foundation? Tell me, if you understand. Who marked off its dimension?"

I read the Bible and I have so many questions. How did Moses know what God said when He was creating the world? How did he know God said, *"Let the land produce living creatures according to their kind?"* How could all of today's population stem from Adam and Eve when we have so many ethnic backgrounds?

Every time I read the Bible, I can find a question that has no answer. So why do I follow this faith called Christianity?

Honestly, for me, it is not about the written word so much as it is about the love behind the word. I know God is real because He has proved himself over and over to me. He has done miracles, answered prayers, and more importantly, has taken up residence in my heart. His spirit dwells within, and I feel Him in there, just as sure as my chest rises and falls when I breathe. There is a peace and a contentment that engulfs me. All is well with my soul. The details and questions that go unanswered do not bother me, because I have something better than answers. I have faith! Faith will carry me through this life and beyond.

I have a few friends who have lost their faith or never really found it. They have questions and need something to physically hold on to in order to believe. But blessed are those who have not seen and yet believe. It is so easy for me to write these words when I have not ever been really tested.

I have questions that may not be answered until I sit by my Father's side and ask them one by one. Until then, I will be content to know that I am not privy to all the answers, and yet I do know that I am loved and adored by the creator of the universe.

Prayer:

Father, I do not need to know all the whys in order to love you. I have your love and that is enough for me. You fill me with your love and peace, and that is all the proof I need.

What are some questions you have about your faith? How important is it that you get the answers? Do you think God is offended by your questioning?

_____

_____

_____

_____

_____

_____

_____

_____

_____

☙ FAMILY ❧

Proverbs 1:8
"...do not forsake your mother's teaching. They will be a garland to grace your head and a chain to adorn your neck."

Does your family play together? Is laughter part of your daily routine? Sometimes I am very amused by my family. We are anything but conventional and boring. Just the other day, I was sitting in our hot tub outside, having a relaxing moment to myself, when all of a sudden—BAM! I got hit in the side of the head with a snowball, compliments of Dale, who was doubled over in laughter. So I repositioned myself to face the other way to keep an eye on him. It was not five minutes later when my daughter and her sleepover company sneaked out the door without my hearing them and jumped up behind me and screamed, scaring the bejeebies out of me! They assumed the same laughing position. So much for a relaxing soak in the hot tub. But all I could do was laugh, because I know I am the reason our family is a family that plays and jokes around. I am the queen of pester, you see. Everyone else has just followed suit. To be honest, I love it! I love dancing the conga through the aisles at the grocery store with my daughter. I love wrestling with my son. I laugh that I could convince the entire family to put a little dab of chocolate on their face at a very nice restaurant. Our waiter totally ignored us, which we found even funnier. To this day, if you ask my children what one of their favorite childhood memories is, they would say the day we had a family ice-cream fight in the kitchen. Now, I do not regret the major cleanup process that took place afterward, because I know we created a memory they will forever cherish.

We laugh, we love, and we play. I hope that when my kids grow up and have families of their own, they will reflect on their youth with appreciation and a great big grin.

Prayer:

Father, thank you for the childlike heart you created in me. Thank you for making me the type of person who does not take life too seriously. Thank you for the family that I adore. I have so much fun with them. Father, thank you so much for the gift of laughter.

What is the funniest memory that you can recall that you had with your family?

_____

_____

_____

_____

_____

_____

_____

_____

_____

❧ FIRST DATES ❧

Ecclesiastes 12:1
"Remember your creator in the days of your youth."

It happened today: My daughter got asked out on her first date. Lucky for me, she has not been one of those boy-crazy teenagers. As a matter of fact, she has not even been that interested in boys up to this point. But now there is someone who caught her eye, and I see a new light and spark coming from her. She smiles more and seems lighter.

I cannot help but reflect on my own first date experience. My first date was with a boy named Glen Hawkins. Boy, did I have a crush on him. He was a great athlete, and I was a little tomboy who was getting her first interest in boys.

We were going to the local fair together, and I was in seventh grade; he was in eighth. As I was waiting nervously for his mother to arrive (she was our driver), I remember looking out the side window of my bedroom, looking down the street, where I had a good view of cars that were coming up the hill. I remember how excited I was when a car would turn the corner and head up the hill, thinking *could that be them?* I was so giddy and excited!

I remember my first date with my first true love.. He was the first guy who really made me nervous. This man rocked my world in a way that threw me off kilter. I was in a dream state all through the date. He dropped me off early with a kiss on the cheek, and I was so enamored with him that I stayed up all night thinking about this guy. I was in love in a big way. First dates, they are truly something to remember.

So this time with Katie seems like a rite of passage for the two of us. I am watching and observing this little girl of mine become a woman. She is such a joy in my life. I want the best for her, and I must admit her date is of good stock. She chose well.

Now comes a new period of time for me. My prayer takes on a different tone. I pray for safety as she rides in the car with boys behind the wheel. I pray for integrity on both sides. I pray for hearts not to be broken. It is somewhat scary because it is all new territory. I know every parent must go through this, but I am not sure we are ever really ready for it.

I am also excited because I get to share in all the fun. I know it somehow makes life worth living, with all of these great, nervous, exciting moments. I have so much to smile about.

Prayer:
Lord, I ask you to please watch over our sons and daughters. Protect their hearts and give them wisdom. Lord, I ask you to prepare the mates you have planned for them. Give them a heart for you and your ways.

Write about your first date, recalling the emotions you felt.

_____

_____

_____

_____

_____

_____

_____

_____

०३ FORGIVEN MUCH ৪০

Luke 7:47
"Therefore, I tell you, her many sins have been forgiven—
for she loved much. But he who has been forgiven little
loves little."

What a precious story! It begins back in verse 36, and you should take a minute and turn there in a Bible to get an overview of the whole story. One of the Pharisees had invited Jesus over to his house for dinner. Jesus was there enjoying His dinner when this woman came in. She was known about town for her wicked ways. When she came in, she fell at Jesus's feet, crying. She had with her this bottle of perfume. As the oil and the tears covered the master's feet, she began to use her hair to dry them. This woman was weary and her heart heavy with shame. She was in need of forgiveness.

Now, the Pharisee was appalled by this woman and thought Jesus did not know of her reputation. But Jesus, in classic form, told a parable and then spoke these words that resonate in my soul: "I tell you, her many sins have been forgiven, for she *loved* much. But he who has been forgiven little loves little."

What this story tells me is this: Those of us who have needed and begged and longed to be forgiven know the value and worth of such an act. We are aware of our need to be forgiven and feel that weight. We also feel the release and the freedom when that forgiveness is granted. Those who think they are not in need of forgiveness do not know the depth of God's wonderful love.

I feel as if God has put inside of me more love than I can contain. After reading these verses, I realize that the love I feel inside has come as a result of forgiveness, for the most part.

You see, I was one who was in need of much forgiveness. I was the woman wiping Jesus's feet with my hair and tears. I have been there. I have felt the love that comes with Jesus saying, "You are forgiven."

Now I stand as one loved beyond what she deserves, and I have a cup that is full and overflowing. I now want to let that same love overflow to the people in my world. That is the beauty of God's love. It just keeps on giving.

Have you ever been forgiven much? Have you ever been in the position that Max Lucado calls "not worthy of the touch of man but worthy of the touch of God?" I have. And His touch healed me and has given me grace with which to love others.

If you have ever been touched by God's grace, you know what I am talking about. It changes you. It teaches you what grace means. It allows you to be nonjudgmental of others. It is a gift birthed out of need and pain, and it is a gift God continues to give.

Prayer:

Lord, time and time again you have picked me up! Boy am I glad you are so strong and have big arms! May I have big arms for the people of my world.

What does the power of God's forgiveness feel like to you?

_____

_____

_____

_____

_____

_____

_____

_____

_____

_____

∞ FRESH GIFTS ∞

2 Corinthians 9:15
"Thanks be to God for his indescribable gift!"

This morning as I sit here to write this devotion, there is something different, something special about today. That something has a name... Burma! She is my new puppy!

I have been waiting so long for the right time and the right dog. She is lying right here beside me, and I can smell that sweet puppy smell, and I can stroke her with my left hand as I write with my other. I am in puppy love. I did not even mind getting up at six o'clock this morning to let her out.

I loved going through the process of picking out dog food and dog toys and dog treats. Even though I spent a small fortune on this puppy, there is nothing like a pet to make you feel like all is well in the world.

I was thinking it is the little gifts like pets that make living on Earth more enjoyable. Pets, mountains, family, friends, Oreos and ice cream are all such great gifts to be thankful for. What are you thankful for today? What really makes your stay here on Earth more enjoyable?

Take time out today to thank God for all those little special gifts that we sometimes take for granted. I think God would appreciate us acknowledging even the smallest of gifts.

Prayer: Thank you, God, for giving us creatures to love and for letting them love us. How odd that an animal can love us so much. It was a nice touch in creation. Thank you.

List some of the little things in life that you really enjoy.

_____

_____

_____

_____

_____

_____

_____

_____

_____

᥍ **FRIENDS** ᕲ

John 15:13
"Greater love has no one than this, that one lay down his life for his friends."

Every year at Christmas, I have a dinner party and I invite the people I consider my very close friends. I get so excited about this evening because it is my night to let each of them know how much they mean to me. I always have treats at their plates, and I have the best time sharing my table, my food, and my home with these wonderful souls. I even smile while preparing the meal. The evening seems magical. When I hear the doorbell ring, I meet my first arrivals with a big hug and kiss and my heart feels so full, and I feel so lucky to have such kind souls surrounding me. If you could measure kindness, my home would be off the Richter scale.

Soon my kitchen is buzzing with chatter and laughter, and I feel as if I must be the luckiest girl in the world. Of course, they have turned my night of tribute to them into a birthday party for *me* (though it isn't until next week)! One of my friends even made me the prettiest cake I have ever seen! That is the perk of having a chef for a friend!

We played games and sang, and I, of course, being me, did not want the night to end. However, long drives awaited my travelers, so I sent them on their way with a silent prayer for safe travels. And I know it will take a few days to get this smile off of my face.

I do not get to see my friends nearly enough. I may see a couple of them only a couple of times a year, but every meeting with them reminds me why I chose to spend the time getting to know them better. They had qualities that I found admirable and a goodness that I was drawn to. To share time with them inspires me to be a better person.

I was thinking about Jesus and what He must have been feeling on the night of the Last Supper. I know His heart must have been so full of love and sorrow that special night. Jesus loved His disciples so much that much of the evening was spent loving them by washing their feet and setting examples for them to follow after He was gone.

I tried to imagine what it would have been like if I had known this was my last meal with my friends. I love them all dearly, but I am sure I am not as close as Jesus was with his posse. I see my friends from time to time, for a few hours at a time. Jesus went on a long camping trip with his buddies and had a relationship that consisted of miracles, teaching, and preparing them to change the world after his departure. That final meal with his close circle had a meaning to the Father that I am sure I cannot comprehend. His last gift to them was to wash their feet and be a servant to them. He was demonstrating giving to the very end of His life.

I hope my friends feel loved by me. I hope that I always act as a servant to them, and most of all, I hope they see Jesus in me.

Prayer:

Lord, please watch over my friends and bless their lives with more goodness than they can contain. Give to them for all they have given to me.

What qualities do you look for in a friend?

_____

_____

_____

_____

_____

_____

_____

_____

_____

❃ GOD OF MIRACLES ❧

Psalms 77:14
"You are the God who performs miracles; you display your power among the people."

One reason why I know my God is real is because of the many ways He answers my prayers. This has been quite a month for answered prayers for me. It all started with a hiking trip gone bad. To begin with it was a long hike and we had got a late start. We then got slightly lost on an overgrown trail, and it began to rain. Soon, darkness was looming and we had to make a decision about what to do. After hiking six and a half miles, we decided to turn around and go back the way we came. We finally made it back down to the truck right at dark. We were hungry, cold, and tired after our thirteen miles. The truck never looked so good to me. Unfortunately, we had left the interior light on in the truck and the battery was dead, and our keys were locked inside the truck. There was a key code on the side of the truck, but it was of no use to us with the dead battery. We were stuck outside in the rain and in the dark.

Our predicament looked like this: We were stuck in a remote area seven miles up a dead-end road on a rainy Sunday night. The chances of someone driving by were slim to none, and slim left town. I was suggesting that we kick in the window and just sleep in the truck for the night. I think my decision was being driven by being cold and tired from the hike. The other option was to walk down the mountain and try to get help from someone at one of the campsites down below. After some deliberation it was decided to start walking down the hill. I grabbed my walking stick and said a quick prayer for help, then turned to hit the street. We did not even take one step on the asphalt before we saw car lights coming up the street, cutting through the fog and rain. A nice couple in a truck stopped and asked if we needed help. We gratefully accepted their offer, and on the long drive back to our house, I asked them what in the world they were doing out that time of night and on that specific road. It seems our rescuers were a couple who have an interesting hobby. They like to hunt down and run over copperhead snakes. They have managed to squish thirty-nine of them this summer, God bless 'em.

They drove us about forty-five minutes up the road to our house and were so good to us. I was, of course, thinking how bizarre the situation was, and thanking God for my little miracle.

A couple of weeks after that situation, I was driving to Nashville and was totally zoned out while driving. I had moved into the slow lane of traffic and spent the first two hours of my drive returning phone calls. When I finished my calls, I just spent that time not thinking about anything heavy and just enjoying the ride. All of a sudden my car died, totally ending my Zen state. I managed to coast off to the side and I looked down to find my gas gauge past empty. I had not even looked at my tank the entire time I was driving. Worse than that, I also had not bothered to pay any attention to any of the exits as I was driving. I had no idea where I was, except to know I was about two hours from home. I saw no mile markers around me, so I figured AAA was going to have their hands full trying to find Waldo. I went to give them a call when I realized— oops—my phone did not have a signal. It is a good thing that I learned a long time ago how to laugh at myself, a trait that has served me well. I got a kick out of my predicament and my lack of attention to the day's driving details. I said a prayer that went something like this: "Okay, God, it looks like I got myself into a mess here. It looks like I cannot fix it on my own, so I could use your help here." With that done, I got out of my truck, tried to look as pitiful as possible, and hoped help would come along soon. Of course, since God was involved, the very next truck stopped—a sand truck, to be specific. The occupant asked if I needed a ride and I gladly accepted. As I pulled myself up by the handle to my seat, I said another prayer for safety with a stranger. The fellow introduced himself to me and he had the radio on. The song playing just happened to be my favorite song "I Can Only Imagine" by Mercy Me. I got a big smile on my face, thinking how God puts His Midas touch on His presence in my life. I believe God purposely put me at ease by not only allowing me to be rescued quickly but by assuring me that my rescuer was a Christian.

Lastly, today at church, I sat beside a woman who recognized me from TV. She introduced herself and we had a brief chat. When church was over, we had a sweet conversation. The church I attend is very large, and it seemed that this sweet woman was having a hard time finding a place to connect there. She felt she had not found her place there yet. So she had said a prayer that morning that God would let her meet someone she knew at church today. I shared with her my own story of when I first started attending there, and it seemed our stories were very similar. Once again God was at work, caring for His children and showing us that we do indeed matter.

Every time God answers one of my prayers, it just causes me to fall deeper and deeper in love with Him. The idea that I matter to a holy God used to be incomprehensible to me. Now it is getting easier and easier for me to accept that the facts speak for themselves. He continually is showing me that He does indeed love me. God is still a God of miracles, so how could I *not* believe?

Prayer:

Father, thank you for being a God of miracles, not only in days gone by, but in this generation as well. Help us, Father, to trust in you and allow you to work in our lives. May you be glorified in your mighty works!

When God presses into your life in a miraculous way, how does that make you feel?

_____

_____

_____

_____

_____

_____

_____

_____

_____

☙ THE HEALING HANDS OF TIME ❧

Romans 5:3-4

"We also rejoice in our sufferings, because we know that suffering produces perseverance; perseverance, character and character, hope."

Have you ever gone through something and thought to yourself, "I am never going to be able to get over or through this?" Then one day you wake up a few weeks, months, or even years down the road and you realize you are on the other side of whatever it was you thought was going to get the best of you. A person, a thought, or an action no longer holds you captive; you are free. If you have never been through something that tough, hold on, because chances are you eventually will go through something difficult. Life has a tendency to throw some zingers at you, usually about the time you think you are pretty well on top of your game.

How dear is the verse about rejoicing in our suffering because it produces perseverance, which produces character, and character produces hope. I do not know if I have ever or will ever rejoice in my suffering, but my trials have proved to me that I can beat whatever comes my way, and one day I will walk on the other side of my problem. I know that for a fact. That does not mean my trials do not hurt me to the core and challenge every fiber of my being, but it does mean that I do have hope. Only through my trials have I been given that gift of belief.

Even now as I write, I am feeling a little relief from a burden that I have been buried under for the past few weeks. I know to just hold on, yet I have been down and blue. Today I woke up and I saw the sun peek through my heart, even though outside it has rained all day. I smiled because again my God was faithful to keep His promise to me.

Prayer:

Father, thank you for loving me when I find it hard to love myself. Thank you for coming to my rescue and building up my strength. These trials are not fun and I hate going through them, but you are building in me something only these trials can build. So I will believe and trust in you.

Recall a time when you were at your lowest. How did persevering through that time change the way you think?

_____

_____

_____

_____

_____

_____

_____

_____

_____

❦ HOW GOD WORKS ❧

Psalms 66:5
"Come and see what God has done, how awesome his works in man's behalf!"

God works in so many different ways in my life. For instance, when I was in need of a pet, I knew not just any dog would do. I knew just the right dog was waiting for me. I had prayed about finding the right dog and I was quite excited to see how this dog would come into our possession. Would it come from my going to the shelter and looking, or from wandering up to our house as a stray, or from knowing someone who knows someone who is giving dogs away? Somehow, some way, I knew I was going to get that pet, and I trusted God with the details.

Sometimes God is a still, small voice. For instance, we were once in a small group that had an interesting beginning. The way it started was I began to run into people who were wounded emotionally. Spiritually, they had taken some pretty hard hits and were really struggling. Over a couple of weeks, it was strange how these people kept running into me. The thought was these people all have a common factor and maybe we should all try to get together. I prayed about it and it seemed God was planting a seed. So I went to the people and asked if they would be interested in forming a small group. All of them jumped at the chance and verified the stirring in my soul at what God was wanting.

Sometimes God is quiet. Oh, this one really bugs me! It is so hard for me to wait on the Lord. Poor Noah. It took him 120 years to build the ark, and surely this whole time he was thinking, "God, are you sure you want me to do this?" He waited and the rains did come. I cannot wait five minutes, for heaven's sake, much less 120 years!

God uses people as well. So many people have spoken truth into my life just when I needed it. Sometimes it is through a book; sometimes through a sermon, and sometimes even a dream. It is amazing to me all the ways God reaches down from heaven to let me know I serve a *great* God!

God will reveal Himself to us at times when we least expect it. One time, I was snow skiing and the resort had a Sunday service on top of a ski slope. I went, and to this day it was the sweetest service I can recall. I felt God's presence stronger than I ever have. That sweet spirit moved across, and as we sang a song of praise, tears were streaming down my face, as I felt I was in the direct presence of a loving God. He showed up on a ski slope!

God's ways of finding us are sometimes unique and sometimes very direct, but the one thing I can say for certain is that you need to pay attention. God does speak to us, but we have to be listening.

Prayer:

God, I must admit I have a lot of questions. I do not know all of the answers, but one thing I do know is that you are alive and well and love me enough to make your presence known in my life.

Think of an occasion God seemed to be crystal clear in what He wanted you to do. What method did He use to reach you?

_____

_____

_____

_____

_____

_____

_____

_____

☙ I CANNOT ESCAPE HIS LOVE ❧

Proverbs 19:22
"What a man desires is unfailing love."

The older I get, the more understanding I gain of this great God I serve. Today I am enthralled by the concept that I cannot chase God away. I am plagued by sin, and my best friend is self-doubt. Guilt or not doing enough haunts me, and yet with all of this, I still feel unbelievably loved by God. His hand reaches past the muck and mire to grab a hold of me and make me feel safe, secure, and important to He who reigns in the place most high. I am amazed and thankful.

The only way I can explain this phenomenon is that it must be like family. You cannot pick your family; you are stuck with what you have. It is the same way with God. God cannot help but love us. It is as if the ability to not love was not programmed into His being.

I can remember a time when I thought I had to act and live a certain way to have God's love. Boy, am I glad I outgrew that way of thinking. If I could get everyone to believe this, I think there would be so much emotional healing in our world. I know it worked wonders for me.

Like rain, His mercy covers me. He serves up tenderness on a silver platter. He kisses the top of my head when I am in His presence. His grip on me is firm and his face is smiling. Do you see God in that same loving type of light? Do you find it hard to believe that He would love you in such a tender way? Trust me when I say I cannot even begin to put into words His tender love for you.

Prayer:

Your love, oh God, is more precious than anything. Help me to see your tender mercy and to understand the way you love your children. Where can I go from your love?

Recall a time in your life when you felt the tender mercy of Jesus.

_____

_____

_____

_____

_____

_____

_____

_____

❧ I REQUIRE MERCY, NOT SACRIFICE ❧

Hosea 6:6
"For I require mercy not sacrifice and acknowledgment of God rather than burnt offerings."

When you have experienced God's mercy firsthand, it tends to make you a more merciful person. Again and again, God has picked me up when I have fallen. He dusts me off, hugs my neck, and pats my backside as He pushes me out the door and says "Try again." I have experienced this love and grace so often now that, when once I feared Him, I now love Him so deeply that I try harder not to fall. That is what love does. It changes you. God does not love only those who do right. I am sure you have heard the comment, "It isn't the well who need the doctor."

The funny thing is, He does not reserve His love for any special group. He loves people who run out of wine at weddings. He loves lepers whose skin is falling off. He loves tax collectors. He even goes to their house for dinner. He loves women caught in adultery. He loves the dead. He loves women who wash His feet with their tears and hair.

He even has a great love for a man who claimed to be His best friend, though he denied Him three times. The God I serve is full of mercy and grace, and He calls me to love the people of my world with this same type of love. What a calling!

To be honest, I can think of at least two people in my life that I just find it really hard to love or forgive. When I think of how easily Jesus loved the unlovely, it motivates me to try harder. He says, "Tina, love your neighbor, and then bring me your sacrifice."

Prayer:

Father, you are my example. You have shown me what true love is, as I have experienced its results. Help me, Father, to love the people in my world that same way.

Name one person that you find hard to love. What makes it hard to love that person?

_____

_____

_____

_____

_____

_____

_____

_____

☾ IT IS JUST STUFF ☽

1 John 2:17
"The world and its desires pass away, but the man who does the will of God lives forever."

My grandmother passed away not long ago, and I had the daunting task of helping my mom and aunt price every item in the house for the estate sale. This woman lived eighty-nine years. You can imagine how much stuff she had accumulated.

When the sale was over and the dust had settled, we counted the dollars and boxed what was left. I looked around at the empty house and was reminded of what I know for sure (as Oprah likes to say). Life is not about getting stuff. If I am going to work for the almighty dollar, I want to spend it on what will last: vacation memories, travel, and adventure. I want to have memories that I can laugh at on my deathbed. I want to spend time with my friends, paying off silly bets like having to do cartwheels down the bowling alley! I want to spend less time at the mall and more time with people who make me laugh.

I have never been much of a shopper, but after the sale, I felt the need to go home and get rid of half of what I had. I want the simple life, with the possessions I have being mostly toys: footballs to pass with my son, Taylor; Frisbees to throw with my daughter, Katie; motorcycles to ride with Dale; tents to sleep in after cooking s'mores and hiking all day; bicycles to ride around Cades Cove loop, which is the prettiest place on Earth.

I want my days to be spent living, and so hopefully when my kids get ready to price all my earthly possessions, it will look more like an outdoor adventure swap meet than an estate sale!

Prayer:

Lord, thank you for all of the "things" you have made available to us. Thank you more that I do not need them in order to be happy.

What are your most prized possessions? What would you buy today if money were of no object?

_____

_____

_____

_____

_____

_____

_____

_____

_____

❧   JESUS MY FRIEND   ❧

Psalms 147:5
"Great is our Lord and mighty in power; his understanding has no limits."

You want to know one of the really cool perks about being a Christian? It is in sharing your every thought with God. Whenever I have questions about what I should do about anything, I usually take it to God. It can be about trivial things that wouldn't matter to anyone else but me—things like what to do with the thirty roses I cut out of my rose garden the other day. I love my roses, but I really did not need that many sitting around the house. So I prayed and asked God to bring to mind anyone who could use a cheerful pick-me-up bouquet. He knows where people are in their life, so I thought the two of us could work together to bring some joy to someone who needed a sweet fragrance in their life that day.

That is the joy of being a Christian. He is always there. He is a great listener. He is trustworthy and He won't tell your secret to anyone. He gives great advice and He seems

to have all the answers. What a friend we have in Jesus...
hey, that sounds like a song!

Prayer:

Father, thank you for being such a reliable friend. You are always there, and I love being able to come and talk to you about everything. You make my life so much better with your sweet presence.

If God was your very best friend, what secrets would you want to share with Him?

_____

_____

_____

_____

_____

_____

_____

_____

_____

_____

☙ LAUGHTER ❧

Proverbs 31:25
"She is clothed with strength and dignity; she can laugh at the days to come."

I love to laugh. I mean to really laugh. You know, the kind when you are laughing so hard that you are not making a sound and the tears come streaming down your face. Or the kind of laughter when you just cannot stop or get control of yourself—like the actors who have to do multiple takes of a scene because they get tickled and then it is next to impossible to get past that scene without falling apart in laughter. Another type of great laughter is when you are passing along a story and, when you get to the point in the story when it gets funny, you just can't get out the last part, and finally everyone is laughing at your laughter, wondering what is so funny. That kind of laughter is a wonderful thing.

Sometimes I get so busy with chores and parenthood that I do not take time to let out a good giggle. Sometimes when I get tickled, I realize how long it has been since I have had a good laugh.

Do not get me wrong; I have a *great* life and I enjoy it. I think sometimes I am just too focused or occupied. Shame on me.

I recently came out of a church service that pulled at every heartstring, and basically I was emotionally spent. I knew I did not want to spend the rest of the day in that condition, so I knew what the cure was: a funny movie. I went to see a comedy and I laughed until I came out a new person. I felt so much better and was grateful for laughter.

So today I am thankful for the Jim Carreys and the Steve Martins of this world. I am so glad they decided not to be corporate executives. They have made my world a better place by being in it. What those guys bring to humanity is of such great value, and it is sometimes underappreciated. So from me to them, spank you very much!

Prayer:

Father, thank you for giving us so much to laugh at. Thank you for a joyful heart, and thank you for your unique makeup of different people. There is need for all different kinds of us.

When was the last time you had a really good laugh? What really gets you tickled?

_____

_____

_____

_____

_____

_____

_____

_____

_____

❈ LIVE AND LET LIVE ❧

John 20:22
"If I want him to live until I return, what is that to you?
You must follow me."

I like this verse because Jesus is basically saying not only to Peter but to all of us, "Butt out of other people's business. I alone am God and the only one who should judge. The only person you need to worry about is yourself and what you are doing."

I may be way off base here, but indulge me for a moment. I think what God meant when He quoted the second greatest commandment, *"love your neighbor as yourself,"* was live and let live. If you have ten cats in your house and that brings you joy, so be it. If you married someone significantly older or younger than yourself, and happily ever after appears to be your destination, then God bless you. Some people have houses full of clutter or knickknacks, while others are neat and minimalist. Some people are socially driven and others are quiet as mice. What about those tired souls called unwed mothers? Some of my friends believe in spanking their children, while others would not dream of it. I even heard of people of different races marrying. Gasp! Can you imagine? Do you want to really push the envelope? How about those people with tattoos and tongue rings? Is there any way you could find it in your being to say, "If they are happy and it works for them, then it is okay by me"?

I think spending time with people from different worlds has helped me realize that I am okay and you are okay. I can live in a world with crazy motorcyclists who like to live on the edge, and I can live with my friends, who think they are the most dangerous machines and won't have anything to do with them. The bottom line to me is that they are all wonderful people with their own opinions.

I enjoy striking up conversations with people who are vastly different from me. I want a glimpse into a world that I seriously doubt I will ever live in. I was at an event one time where I saw a gentleman who had a face full of piercings. What was not pierced was tattooed, and though his outward appearance was a little intimidating, I decided to go sit next to him and ask him a few questions about himself. It was not long before he was taking his shirt off for me and showing me the rest of the story his body told through his tattoos. He was such a nice guy, even if he was vastly different from me.

I have a plaque at my house that states, *"People are like books, each with their own story to tell. I wonder how many books can I read and how many books can I love?"* I love that statement. Right now, I am sitting on a plane next to a gentleman who looks to be in his mid-thirties. He is reading a comic book. I do not think I have ever read a comic book in my whole life. I am curious what his interest is in the comic world. I hope to finish writing this chapter in time to ask him a few questions about himself. Some would think it odd that a grown man is reading comics. I mean, after all, life is so serious, and couldn't his time be better spent? But what I am thinking is there is a world I am totally uneducated about, and I would like to learn what the interest is.

Wouldn't it be nice if all of us could get to a place in life that we could stop thinking that other people are weird or wrong if they are not just like us? Freedom can be found in realizing that things do not have to be right or wrong; they can just be. Along this same line of thinking, let's cut people some slack about choices they have made. Haven't we all made mistakes? I try really hard not to ever judge people or mistakes they have made. I refuse to say or even think "shame on you." Instead, my heart aches for the pain they must have had to live with. I think most of us beat ourselves up pretty well. We do not really need more help from our fellow man. Yet that seems to be what we are best at doing. I may not agree with or even understand the road you have traveled, but the most loving thing I could do would be to love you and help you find a path that will be less painful.

It was during a very empty time that I read a story wherein God healed a leper. All had forsaken the leper, and it was not a man who reached out to him. Jesus was the one who physically touched the man. Jesus could have healed him with His words but chose to do it with a touch. I have felt like that leper, not worthy of the touch of man but worthy of the touch of God. That lesson taught me two things. One was to never make a person feel untouchable, and the second was that God will never forsake us.

Prayer:

God, teach us to be graceful with our fellow humans. Why do we want to run each other into the ground for being different? Help us, Lord, to learn to celebrate differences and learn about the people behind the things we find strange.

In what area of your life do you feel like you could be more grace filled?

_____

_____

_____

_____

_____

_____

_____

_____

_____

❧ MAKING A DIFFERENCE ❧

Mark 10:31
"But many who are first will be last, and the last first."

I want you to think for a moment on this question: Have you ever made a difference in someone else's life? I think that is the real reason we are all here: to help each other. When I am lucky enough to make a difference in someone else's life, it somehow gives purpose and meaning to my own. It makes the everyday rituals seem important. Could it be you are here on Earth not for yourself but for someone else? Maybe even ten someone elses. What if God wants to use you today to get a message across to someone else? Will you do it? Will you even know God wants to use you? Are you quiet and still long enough for God to tell you?

I love the movie *Pay it Forward*. It is a feel-good movie about a random act of kindness being passed on and on. It shows the good side of us humans. If we would only quit living for just ourselves, it is amazing how many people we might be able to change or help. I do not want to leave this planet having lived only for me. I want more. I want to feel as if I am doing more than just taking up space.

The second greatest commandment was to love your neighbor as yourself. That right there tells me that it is more important to serve the people in my world than for me to do most anything else.

I love the verse "I require mercy, not sacrifice." Oh how we like to think that we can work our way into heaven. I bet, if we could look into the heart of God, we would see that He smiles more when we forgive or when we extend mercy to the "least of these." I think that is what God wants from His people—for us to just help each other get by.

Prayer:

Father, you said, "The last shall be first." I believe that to be true. I never feel higher than when I choose to serve others. Help us, Father, to think of others more than we do ourselves.

Who is someone you could help, even if it was in a small way?

_____

_____

_____

_____

_____

_____

_____

_____

_____

☙ MENTORS ❧

1 Timothy 4:12
"Don't let anyone look down on you because you are young, but set an example for the believers in speech, in life, in love, in faith, and in purity."

This is my son's favorite verse. He is only seventeen years old, but he knows the importance of setting an example for others to follow. Is there someone in your life who you look up to, or someone who just seems to have it all? They are balanced and happy, and life seems as if it comes easily for them.

When I first became a Christian, I began to listen to Chuck Swindoll on the radio. I also started reading everything that he wrote. He molded and shaped the way I thought. If Chuck said it, I believed it. He taught me that you do not have to be a sourpuss to be a Christian. He also taught me about character and handling failure. He even gave me the two thumbs up on getting a motorcycle. Chuck Swindoll helped mold me into the Christian that I am today.

Isn't it amazing how powerful a life can be? Chuck probably will never know how much of an influence he has been in my life. I have never seen or spoken to the Sermonator in the twenty-eight years he has been shaping my life. If I ever get to meet the man, I would like him to know how much I admire and respect him.

My son currently has a mentor. He is Taylor's Young Life leader. This young man spent a large amount of time with the kids, eating lunch with them at school, attending their sports events on the weekends, taking the guys to the lake, picking them up or dropping them off if they didn't have a ride somewhere. As a matter of fact, this young man just changed colleges in order to go into the ministry. Taylor really looks up to this guy. He is being shaped and molded by this mighty mentor. I am so thankful for this mentor, and I pray a bounty of blessings on him for how he chooses to use his time.

Mentors—what would the world be without them? I am thankful for my mentor. How about you? Take time today to tell your mentor or someone who has made a difference in your life how much he or she means to you.

Prayer:

Father, one of your greatest blessings in my life has been a mentor. I cannot thank you enough for his example in my life. I ask for an extra dose of blessings on my friend's life today. Help me to understand the power of being a mentor and pass on the same gift to someone else.

Who is your mentor? What impact has this person had on your life?

_____

_____

_____

_____

_____

_____

_____

_____

_____

☛ MOMENTS OF REVELATION ☚

Exodus 31:13
"This will be a sign between me and you for the generations to come, so you may know that I am the Lord, who makes you holy."

I love having my quiet time in the morning. I cannot tell you how many times I have had moments of revelation during this time. It usually comes from one of my readings. Today it came from the book *I Promise You a Crown* by Julian of Norwich. This great woman lived in the 1300s and had what we would call today a life-or-death experience. She writes of her visions and of how they were understood.

Today's topic was on God's unceasing love. I was brought up to believe that I must see my sin and turn away from it, and *then* God's anger is turned away and we can be forgiven and experience His mercy. Julian saw a different type of love in her holy meeting with the master. What she saw was there was no holding back on God's love for us. She said, "It seemed impossible that God, who is love, could withhold any part of love for us until after we turn to Him. I saw only love. Instead, God produces a longing for peace, a longing for freedom from restlessness. And by working within us (which we call grace), He brings us to rest. He works in us, and He does so to reveal our own dissatisfaction to us."

Oh, that is good stuff! How I can relate! I get sick and tired of being restless and not at peace. That sick and tired brings me to my knees. I desire fellowship with God, who loves me. I miss Him if we are not in fellowship. How sweet to go to Him out of love instead of having to in order to get a needed response.

Prayer:

Father, thank you for how you work in our lives. Thank you for not holding out on your love for us. You are amazing and it is your amazing love that draws me to you. It is your grace that pulls me away from sin and into your waiting arms.

Do you have to do everything right for your parents to love you? If God's love for us is so much greater than human love, then why do we still think that we have to earn His love? Write your thoughts about what it takes for God to love you.

_____

_____

_____

_____

_____

_____

_____

_____

_____

☙ MOTHERS AND DAUGHTERS ❧

Isaiah 49:15
"Can a mother forget the baby at her breast and have no compassion on the child she has borne?"

I recently hosted a Christmas mother/daughter cookie swap. What a precious memory and sweet time I had. My redheaded friend since the age of three came with her two daughters, who are now sixteen and thirteen. Boy did that make me feel old.

Before swapping cookies, I had all the moms go around and say something they love about their daughters. Then the daughters got their chance to tell of something they appreciate about their moms.

I was very moved by the love shared between all of the women in the room. I was reminded how no one can give a mother's love to a daughter except for her mother. I also saw the need for daughters to love their mothers, and how valued that is among us moms.

As long as there have been mothers who have produced daughters, there has been a mother/daughter bond that has ranged somewhere between intolerable and best friend. I do not know a single girl whose relationship with her mother is not important. If it is good, they value it. If it is not, they wish they had a richer relationship. The reason for that is simply that we girls need our moms. They cannot be replaced, and there is no other relationship that can fill those shoes.

Mothers provide a comfort that no one else can give. They give us wisdom that only mothers have. A mother knows us because she has paid attention to every detail of life. She is our confidant and our babysitter, our hair stylist and our conscience.

My mother passed on to me great quotes like, "You can't keep birds from flying around your head, but you can keep them from building nests in your hair." I also liked, "Oh what a tangled web we weave when first we practice to deceive." My mom taught me about men when I became a new bride, telling me that a man's ego is very fragile and to never attack it. She gave me a love for music. She was the best person in the world to learn from about cooking and party planning.

My mom has been an invaluable asset to my life. Even though I usually choose to do things my way and screw up rather than to be told what to do or do it someone else's way, I still hear her voice in my head at all times. That must be another mother skill: transferring her voice into our heads, so no matter where we go or what we do, she is somehow there and we think about what our mother would do or say. Hey, maybe they should market a WWMS (What would Mother say?) bracelet!

Prayer:

Lord, what would we do without our moms? They are a gift that cannot be measured. They are a treasure that we cannot fully appreciate. Thank you for mine.

What are the best qualities about your mother?

_____

_____

_____

_____

_____

_____

_____

_____

_____

❧ OLDER BUT NOT OLD ❧

Job 12:12
"Is not wisdom found among the aged? Does not long life bring understanding?"

A couple of years ago, I took a "real age" test. I have always known that I do not feel or act my age. The result of the test was that my real age was twenty-seven. That is the good news. The bad news is I must work a little harder these days at feeling youthful. Gone are the days of eating Cinnabons whenever I want. I have also noticed that I seem to ache a little more and longer after a workout.

The older I get, the more I take note of people in their golden years. Some are bitter and some are hateful, and then there are some who shine. My papaw Thrasher is ninety-one years young. He is so full of vim and vigor, and I love to be with him. I like watching and listening to how he treats other people. My papaw tries to treat everyone special, and he is very kind.

My life has been blessed with old-age examples. I want to be a giggler like G.G. Collins was. I want to be the one to put a twinkle in other people's eyes like my papaw Thrasher.

I may be a little premature in my thinking, but I am just watching and planning ahead. When I go down to Florida, I play volleyball with a group of people who vary in age from fifty to eighty. These folks are very happy and fun to be around. They laugh and make fun of each other and make all of us visitors feel welcome. One eighty-three-year-old lady takes the tai chi class and even line dances. These fine folks make me glad that I woke up and got to be a part of their world.

Another youthful elder is my friend Victor who just turned ninety. This man still drives and is sharp as a tack. He is so playful that he still has all sorts of playful contests for his grown children. I bet if he took that real age test he would be around fifty or sixty.

My father-in-law is seventy-nine and he still gets up at 3:30 in the morning to go to the market and sell produce. He works his own garden and loves every minute of it. By looking at him, you would not think he is a day over sixty. He remains a youthful and handsome man.

I can promise you one thing: I am not going to take getting older lying down. I am going to suck every drop out of life that I can. I am not going to be the one sitting in my rocking chair saying I wish that I had done this or that. I am living every day as if it is my last, and I suggest you do the same.

If you know someone who seems fully alive though they are in their golden years, why not take a few minutes out of your day to let them know that you notice their positive attitude. I think they need to know that they are encouraging us to not grow old while we are growing older.

Prayer:

Lord, thank you for all the people who have shown me how to age by their example. I ask you to bless all those who refuse to go down without a fight. Let me learn by their example. Then when I am old, let me be the same example for someone else.

What senior citizen could you encourage today by telling them they how special they are?

_____

_____

_____

_____

_____

_____

_____

_____

◌ঁ PARENTING ৪০

Proverbs 22:6
"Train up a child in the way he should go, and when he is old he will not turn from it."

Oh boy, have I done it this time. I do not know what I was thinking when I had two children thirteen months apart. I should have known that there would come a time when I would have two teenagers living under the same roof. So right now I am dealing with all the issues that a seventeen-year-old boy goes through, and I have a girl experiencing her first semester of college. What do you do when the car is taken out without permission or Spanish remains a foreign language to your child and they fail? Granted, it is easier now than it was having a junior and senior in high school. It may also be better than it was having two middle schoolers. But one thing is for sure: It has never been a simple task. How in the world something so difficult can be so rewarding is a mystery to me.

I am reading a book on how to raise teenage boys, and though I know it is a great responsibility, I am going to force myself to enjoy this time. I only get one chance at this and I want to be fully in this moment. It is very daunting to know that I could potentially say or do something that could leave a scar on my child emotionally. I only hope and pray that they show me the same mercy that I have shown to them.

I believe that, to be a good parent, it is wise counsel to remember what it was like when you were a youth. I think it is wrong to expect your children to somehow be more mature or responsible than you were. We are all the same when it comes to having to go through the growing-up process. It is good to remember that they are children sometimes packaged in grown-up bodies.

Some people have had more responsibilities laid on them in their youth than others. Those people tend to be a little more serious and have less time for the foolishness and youthful things. You know you are in the presence of one of those people when you get the lecture that starts out something like "When I was a kid, we did not have all the things that you did. We were too busy milking the cows and planting the fields, or…"

Do not get me wrong. I do not believe that I have all the parenting answers, but I do know that I try as hard as I can to be fair. At the time I am in the crisis of the moment, I am not too together. But give me a little time to cool off and I am back to smiling at the pleasure of raising two great kids! I think I do well at putting things into perspective. It takes a lot to really rock my boat. Life is for living, and personally, I was never one to be devastated by a C in Spanish. I hope in the end my children will think that I was fair, that I protected them, and that there were many more good memories than bad.

Prayer:

Father, give all of us parents wisdom. If you do not mind, throw in an abundance of patience and some unconditional love. Teach us how to listen to our children with ears that truly hear what they are trying to tell us, even when they aren't speaking.

What did you do right in parenting? Where do you feel you fall short?

_____

_____

_____

_____

_____

_____

_____

_____

_____

☙ PINK HAIR ❧

Psalms 146
"I call out to you; save me..."

When I get to the end of this life, I hope I can go out with a feeling of no regret. So far I feel pretty good about how I have gone about things. Even when I made choices that were not necessarily right ones, I believe that they served a purpose, and I would not take any of it back. Sometimes I think the experience is what matters, not necessarily the outcome. If given the choice to trade lives with anyone else, I would gladly refuse the offer.

If I had a do-over, the only thing I might choose is to just say no when my daughter asked if I wanted to put pink stripes in my hair with her. That mother/daughter bonding moment turned into weeks of permanent, bright, cotton-candy-pink stripes in my forty-five-year-old hair. For some reason, it didn't look nearly as ridiculous on her eighteen-year-old locks.

I did try to bleach out the pink (the only option for the mess I had gotten myself into), however, that only dulled the brilliance. The end result was it just had to wear off, which took several weeks. I had to endure more than one "What were you thinking?" comment.

It is a good thing I do not take myself too seriously. I can laugh at some of the stupid things I have done. Luckily, most of my "boy that was stupid" moments did not have serious repercussions, which is why, for now, I can say quite thankfully: no regrets.

Prayer:

Lord, thank you for the great first half of my life. There have been so many more good times than bad, and for that I am grateful. I pray for a life lived fully—complete, with no regrets.

What is something you regret? Did anything good come of it?

_____

_____

_____

_____

_____

_____

_____

_____

_____

○ঃ PURITY ৪০

Psalms 51:1-7
"Cleanse me with hyssop, and I will be clean; wash me, and I will be whiter than snow."

Last night before I went to bed, the weatherman warned of a cold front coming through that should dump some snow on our little corner of the world. Hundreds of other mothers like me prepared by buying out our local grocer, in case it snowed for the next month! Then we went to bed, hoping that when we woke up, our world would look a little whiter. Like a child, I awoke from my slumber and went to the window, and I stared I in awe at the beauty of the snow. The trees were bent from the weight of the powder resting on their limbs, and everywhere I looked, everything was uniformly colored. There were no contrasting gray streets or green grass. It made me aware of the significance of the statement "pure as the driven snow." My world looked peaceful, pure, and perfect.

I wish my soul looked like that. I have always wanted to please my heavenly Father. If I could be perfect for Him, I would because I love Him so much. Try as I may, I am not made of snow but of flesh and blood, and my flesh does not have much in common with the pure snow. I fail and I fall short, and I begin to look more like the sludge that piles up on the side of the road after two or three days.

The good news is that I dare to trust that God loves us as we are. We do not have to be perfect or close to it in order to have His love. His love is greater than we imagine. We tend to limit God to our own humanistic limitations. But the fact is that God loves me just as I am. So just like I love the world I live in, even when the snow is not around, he loves me, pure or not. As a matter of fact, we only get one or two snows a year. And I am sure there are moments of goodness in me, but for the most part, I am simply human, with all the limitations that come from that.

I am so thankful that my God is greater and more loving than this girl can comprehend. Brennan Manning says, "If you think you can comprehend God's love then that is not God because His love is incomprehensible. So think again." I like that. That means that, no matter how loving I think my God is, He will always be more than that! What a concept.

Prayer:

Thank you, Father, for making my world look a little different today. Lord, how I wish that I could be that pure. I invite you to work through me to purify me so I can be that beautiful to you.

Write a word picture for what you think God sees when He looks at you.

_____

_____

_____

_____

_____

_____

_____

_____

_____

♋ PURPOSE ♌

Ephesians 3:11
"according to his eternal purpose which he accomplished through Jesus Christ our Lord."

We were talking as a family last night at the dinner table about what our purpose may be while we are here on this planet. My son Taylor thought his purpose was to share laughter and joy with people. He is Mr. Up! He is never in a bad mood and is just a delight to be around. He brings fun into most every situation.

My daughter Katie thought her purpose was to share beauty with the world. She is quite artistic. She paints and makes collages and is just so creative. She is also very kind and is going to be a great mate to someone down the road.

My purpose is to love the people of my world—all people, especially the unlovable ones. (Is there such a thing?) The more the world has rejected a person, the more I want to show them they have value and worth. I have so much inside that I want to give.

What is your purpose? Do you feel as if you were created to give something to the world? Do you ever stop and think that God made you with a specific thing in mind to bring to the world? He is counting on you to use that special gift He gave you to go out and share it in your school, community, home, or workplace. So what are you waiting for? Get out there and shine in your own light.

Prayer:

Lord, thank you for loving us so much that you would make us all uniquely different. May I use the gift that you gave to me to bring joy to someone. I just might be what someone else needs today.

What do you think your purpose is in life?

_____

_____

_____

_____

_____

_____

_____

_____

❧ REACHING OUR MOUNTAINTOPS ❧

James 1:4

"Perseverance must finish its work so that you may be mature and complete, not lacking in anything."

Nothing inspires me more than to see someone succeed at something that was difficult for him or her to do. That may be why I enjoy watching *Fear Factor*. It is all about overcoming your fears and just doing it. I get a rush just watching the contestants succeed at their challenges.

My good friend just finished her last class in college. She is graduating at the ripe old age of thirty-six. She has worked and been self-supporting since she was seventeen years old. She took classes one or two at a time when she could, and now here she is graduating. I am so proud of her.

This last weekend my daughter, mom, and dad went on a hike with me. It was a difficult hike. It was only two miles, but it was straight up the entire way. For me to do this was not really a big deal, but for them to do this was more than impressive to me. They are not the athletic, outdoor type. My daughter does not even like the out of doors. (I am convinced that it was God's sense of humor to give me a child like this.) Yet both of them made it to the top and climbed out on the rocks to view the world two miles above it. I was amazed and very proud as they stood on their perch, overlooking the Great Smoky Mountains as their reward.

I wonder if God feels this same way when we resist a temptation or we succeed at a trial. I have a feeling that our heavenly Father smiles when we reach our mountaintops or take our final classes. Come to think of it, that is basically all life is: a series of tests and trials. We either pass or fail. We either make it to the top of that mountain or we turn around and go back.

How are you doing with your tasks? Are you growing in your strength and feeling as if your past trial victories are pulling you up that mountain, or are you on your hands and knees, crawling up? Maybe you have not given up but are not quite sure you have what it takes to get up that mountain. Hold on; keep fighting the good fight. Remember, every one of these battles you get into is only making you a stronger warrior!

Prayer:

Lord, help me up my mountains. Be my strength and courage. I am not afraid of these tests and trials, Lord. I know my life will be full of them. I only desire to make you smile as I pass the test and make it up my mountain.

Recall a mountain you had to climb in your personal life. How did you do with the process?

_____

_____

_____

_____

_____

_____

_____

_____

☞ RESTLESSNESS ☜

Psalms 103:14
"For he knows how we are formed…"

Thank goodness God does not have a recall program on His creations. I am sure that he may have been in a silly mood when He mixed the genes in my mother's womb. If you have ever heard the saying "she has ants in her pants," that is me. I am constant motion. Yoga is totally out of the question for me. The worst part of my childhood had to be the naps I was subjected to, which now I am convinced were more for my mother's sanity than my good.

Idleness is my worst enemy. I become evil if I do not have something to do. It is this restlessness that also drives me to adventures, that keeps me in shape, and that makes me a fun mom. On the flip side of all of this, it is a curse. It makes me a horrible person to live with if I get stuck too long in a car or inside my house for more than a day. On a few occasions, I have been sick and I told my family, "Just shut my door, and when I feel better, I will come out." I am not looking for sympathy, just brighter days.

I also tend to get restless with ordinary days. At least I used to. I am about cured of that sickness since traveling so much, because of my new career. I got to a point that I was craving the ordinary days that I used to complain about. At times, I get tired of all the madness and I hit the road on my motorcycle, where there are no phones and no passengers. Oh how I love those days. It feels like freedom. My restlessness subsides and I go back home to cook supper with my face still tingling from the wind rushing past it all day.

I guess it is okay being the way I am. God did make me unique, I believe. Restlessness drives me to do more in a day than should be legal, and it allows me the creativity to say, "Let's eat spaghetti without forks tonight." On the rare occasion that I cannot find on outlet, it gives me a chance to thank God that usually I can!

Prayer:

Lord, I am a restless soul, a butterfly with constantly flapping wings, darting from here to there. My mind is constantly stuck in the on position as well. Knowing this about myself helps me to choose healthy way to fulfill that restless spirit. Help me to know when that spirit is getting in the way of my being kind to those I love.

What is one of your not-so-great qualities? Is there a way
you can use it for the good?

_____

_____

_____

_____

_____

_____

_____

_____

_____

ℭ **SERVING** ℭ

Philippians 2:5-7
"Your attitude should be the same as that of Christ Jesus:
Who, being in very nature God, did not consider equality
with God something to be grasped, but made himself
nothing, taking the very nature of a servant."

Something came across my e-mail today that was so
simple yet so profound. It was speaking about crayons and
how some are sharp, some are dull, some are bright colors,
while others are not so brilliant. The interesting thing is
that all of the different crayons all get along together in
the same little box. How I wish that we as people could do
that. There are so many non-acceptances in our world. The
Christians and the non-Christians sometimes resent each
other. Some blacks and whites still have a wall between
them. A lot of straights and gays continue to bicker.

Our society is competitive in nature. Everyone seems to
be trying to get ahead or above everyone else. We want to
get that position at work and hope the guy beside us does

not. We hire people based on their color. We choose our friends based on their social stature. We buy stuff so that it looks like we are somebody. Something has gone terribly wrong in our world.

I was in a 10k race one Saturday morning, and as I was running, I noticed that a runner had fallen. Another runner had stopped to help the runner, and I was shocked to see who it was who had come to this runner's aid. It was a woman who trains almost every day. Running has been her passion. She places in most all of her races because this little lady is fast! I am sure that on race day, her thoughts were on running her best time or placing high in the race. By stopping to help this poor soul, she forfeited her place and her prize. That is being a servant at its best.

What if, instead of trying to get ahead, we tried helping other people get ahead? What if we put others first, humbled ourselves, and became the servants we are called to be? I wonder what our world would look like if we all chose this type of living. I know this is just wishful thinking. I cannot change the world, but I can change me.

Prayer:

Lord, what I would not give to live in a world of love and to live in harmony with my fellow man. I want to be a spreader of your love and grace. Help me, Lord, to learn how to be a better servant to the people of my world.

What could you do to be a better servant?

_____

_____

_____

_____

_____

_____

_____

_____

_____

⊗   SILENT REBEL   ⊗

Ephesians 6:12
"For our struggle is not against flesh and blood, but against the rulers, against the authorities, against the powers of this dark world and against the spiritual forces of evil in the heavenly realms."

A counselor once called me a silent rebel. You know the type: those who are pleasers, yet there is some mischief down there hiding. The truth of the matter is that two words could not have better described me. Let me give you an example. To the horror of purists and my mother, I have two tattoos. That is the rebel side of me. The silent side of me got them where no one would ever see them.

I must admit that, if my life were full of simple conflicts like this, I would be fine with living this dual personality. The problem comes when it feels more like a battle between flesh and spirit. Unfortunately, I am not protected from the age-old battle. The silent rebel in me is in true form. Daily,

I have to make choices, I have to silence thoughts, and I have to fight selfishness.

I have learned that I need to have my quiet time in the mornings just to give me a jumpstart over my flesh. If I start my day with filling my heart and mind with Christ, then I have a better chance at winning some of the battles I know my day will hold. This is my favorite part of the day: sitting with my Savior and learning more of Him, and resting from battle. When I am done, I am armored up and ready to go. I am ready to try and live victoriously with the rebel who will always be part of me.

Prayer:

Father, you know me. You made me high-spirited, adventurous, and restless. Now with your help, I must channel all of this for the good. You are growing me, but I must do my part. Help me, Father, to honor you with the person you created me to be.

Do you take time to sit and be still with God? How does it benefit you?

_____

_____

_____

_____

_____

_____

_____

_____

_____

෫ SLOW TO ANGER ෨

James 1:19-20
"My dear brothers, take note of this: Everyone should be quick to listen, slow to speak and slow to become angry, for man's anger does not bring about the righteous life that God desires."

I have adopted a mentality over the last few years that seems to be working pretty well for me. I have decided to listen more and talk less. This little shift in behavior has seemingly changed all my relationships for the better. I still get frustrated and a little irritable at times but am learning to keep my trap shut until things settle down a little. Being slow to speak has saved me from having to say I'm sorry more times than I care to admit.

Have you ever had one of those days when everything gets under your skin? I hope you say yes. Misery loves company. I guess we all are subject to bad days, but the prize goes to the one who gets through it without taking victims into its avalanche.

Personally, I know when I am in one of those moods when everything seems to be getting under my skin. I have learned on those days to own up to my irritability and announce it to family. Sometimes I will apologize for my mood up front, and my son takes that on as a personal challenge to make me laugh. That is his gift. If his skills do not work, then I try to react by not reacting to things, but reflecting instead. I will take a minute before I open my mouth to say anything.

I like what my daughter says when she encounters someone being angry or hateful. She will say, "You need a mommy very badly," quoting a line from her favorite movie, *Hook*.

The bottom line is, I know that I cannot always control my mood, because I have hormones that do not ask for permission to act up. I do, however, have control over how I let myself respond to what is going on inside of my body. I am not perfect and fall short often, but at least I am aware and try my best to keep my tongue where it belongs…in my mouth!

Prayer:

Father, forgive me when I do not reflect you. Today I was anything but you. Thank you for being patient and giving me chance after chance to improve.

How do you respond to anger? How could you improve the
way you react when you are frustrated?

_____

_____

_____

_____

_____

_____

_____

_____

_____

_____

cs **SOARING** so

Acts 7:49
"Heaven is my throne, and the earth is my footstool."

I am one of those types of people who see the glass as half-full instead of half-empty. I also like to make lemonade out of lemons. One of the lemons in my life is that, due to circumstances surrounding my adoption, I tend to be a detached type of person. I am more of a loner and I honestly enjoy doing many of my activities alone. That does not mean that I do not love and love deeply. It simply means that I prefer to run by myself. I love to take long walks and ride my bicycle by myself. I enjoy hitting a movie matinee alone. I am sure there are some people who will not go out to dinner or do much of anything else unless they have someone to do it with, but that is not who I am. I seem to find more peace in being alone than I do by being around other people. That is not right or wrong; it just is.

Nothing in this world has a hold of me—not money, things, power, or a career. I am a free spirit in the purest sense. This is why, when I put on my headphones and ride my bike or run, I can sing loudly and feel no ties to this earthly place. I can soar with my heavenly Father in His presence. I do not feel at home here on this planet. I feel free from earthly ties and bonds. I honestly feel that my time on earth is just a temporary stop for me. I enjoy my time here and I certainly take advantage of everything it has to offer, but it does not own me and I do not own it.

In order to be truly free, you must not have chains that bind you. Some people are so busy chasing the almighty dollar that they are not even aware that soaring is a possibility. Some are so busy climbing to that top rung of the ladder that they cannot even enjoy the world outside of the office. One of my close friends says it best: "We work so hard to get the things that we do not have time enjoy." Many folks are so busy wanting what they do not have that they cannot enjoy the things they do have.

One thing I have noticed is that the older people get the more they realize that happiness does not come in acquiring material things. Have you ever gone shopping with your grandmother? First of all, she probably will not want to go shopping, and secondly, if she does go, she won't buy anything, because she just doesn't need it. Our grandparents usually do not live in big houses either. As we age, we begin to scale down. We want to simplify our lives and get rid of the stuff we had to have in our youth. I believe that this freedom from the material world is what makes our grandparents seem so at peace in the world. If we are going to soar, we have to first let go off all that binds us.

Prayer:

    I am a unique creation. I soar with you to places this world cannot match. Nothing contains my spirit or has me held to this place. I am free.

What really makes you soar?

_____

_____

_____

_____

_____

_____

_____

_____

♋ THE BEST OF TIMES, THE WORST OF TIMES ♌

Proverbs 27:1
"Do not boast about tomorrow, for you do not know what a day may bring forth."

This crazy life we live in is so full of change. It is hard to maintain one thought or one constant habit because it is always changing. You may get in the habit of doing your exercise in the morning, then bang—all of a sudden, your mother falls ill and you have to run over to her house every morning.

You may be used to family dinners and talking around the dinner table, sharing each other's day. Then, all of a sudden, your kids get older, you trade the chef hat in for being a taxi driver, and you have to eat at drive-thru for the next few years.

Life can be coasting along so well and your world is a happy place. All seems balanced and well in life, and then you are hit with a death, a sickness, a divorce, a pregnancy, a financial setback, or just plain ol' loneliness may set in. The next thing you know, you find yourself in the dumps and yet it seems like just yesterday you were singing God's praises. Somehow, before you know it, all the turmoil quiets down, and you find your smile again, and gone is the rain.

I must admit, I am very fortunate that during most of my time spent here on Earth, I have been in the smiling place. There have been some bumps along the way that took me to knees, but for the most part I try to seek the good in things. I can usually gauge where I am in life by looking at my prayer list. In the *general* section, there are some heavy requests that cause a little anxiousness, such as praying for our president. Second is praying for all the soldiers and their families as they deal with the separation and the anxiety of war. When I move to the *personal* page, I see the biggest cause for concern on that list is a prayer for a puppy. Do we, don't we? Big or small? My heart says yes; my mind says no. Oh Lord, what am I to do?

I am so thankful for this time in my life. I told myself this morning "These are the days!" I can see myself looking back one day and remembering this exact place I am in. All is well with my soul. My children are happy and healthy. Financially, we are secure and have no worries there. I seem to be living in a perfect world. But I know it will not last. Life cannot be stopped or put on hold. Things are going to happen in the future. I think it is these "good times" that pull you through the bad times. When turmoil hits, you remember the days of laughter and long for them. Personally, I seek them out. I choose joy. I try to find it even in the hardest of times. I look for positives in any given situation, and I find my refuge there. Even in my worst times, I found comfort in just reminding myself that tomorrow is another day.

Prayer:

Lord, thank you for this beautiful place I am in. Let me never take for granted these times. Burn this memory into my heart and mind, to reflect upon when the storms do come. May I never forget from where my blessings flow.

Recall a time in your life when everything seemed right and when everything seemed wrong.

☙ THE CHANGING TIDE ❧

Psalms 73:23
"Yet I am always with you; you hold me by my right hand.
You guide me with your counsel."

I am reminded today of a period in my life I would just as soon forget. The best word to describe me would have been *restless*. Everything in my life was in chaos. My marriage was faltering, my health was restricting my physical activities, I had lost my joy and zeal for life, and nothing fulfilled me. I was in counseling at the time, and my counselor told me that I was so discontented that if I died and went to heaven, I would still be dissatisfied. The words stung, and yet I knew he was right.

I was off-kilter, unhappy, unbalanced, and unhealthy. I was a restless shell roaming the Earth looking for relief. Ever been there? Like Mick Jagger, I couldn't get no satisfaction. I can say from experience that it is not a pleasant place to be.

When I compare those years (at least three really bad ones) to my life now, I wonder how I ever endured it. Yet, now looking back on it, I am somehow thankful for them.

It is because of the bad times that I really cherish and value these good times. I look back and know the realness of a less-than-happy life.

The only other good to be found in reflecting upon that period of my life is that I can look into the eyes of someone who is going through the same sort of emptiness, and speak truth to them out of experience.

My words are those of hope alone. I say, "Hold on. Things will get better. Maybe not this year, but eventually you will see the sun shine again. Do not give up or give in to the pain." Sometimes holding on is all we can do. It is comforting to some degree to know that God is there with you, holding your hand, and that He will *never* leave you. That is His promise to us all.

Looking back, I realize I had to make some personal changes in my personal life that were extremely difficult and came at a great price. Then I just had to wait, hold on, and let time pass.

Now here I am at one of the happiest times of my life. Oh, how the tides have changed. I now know that, if the storms return and I am being tossed by the storm, clear skies are on the way, and I just have to wait out the storm.

If you are currently in a low place and find it hard to face another day, my plea to you is to just hold on. Pray to a loving God who knows your pain, and trust that the sun will shine again.

Is there anything you need to do to help that change come about? As the saying goes, "If you do what you've always done, you will get what you always gotten."

If you are at a good place right now and everything seems to be working, thank God for each and every moment! I do!

178   *Tina Wesson*

Prayer:

Father, life is always changing and I thank you for the good times and the bad. I live in such a state of gratitude these days. You are so good to us all, and it is amazing how you use the times of despair to reach others. Thank you for your promise of brighter days!

When times are tough, what drives you to keep your head up and keep going?

_____

_____

_____

_____

_____

_____

_____

_____

_____

ଓ THE LEAST OF THESE ଅ

Colossians 3:12
"Therefore, as God's chosen people, holy and dearly loved, clothe yourselves with compassion, kindness, humility, gentleness and patience."

There are so many "least of these" that I have had the privilege of being acquainted with. One such gentleman was named Will.

Will worked for Goodwill Industries. He was the attendant at the drop-off trailer in Kroger's parking lot. Season after season, year after year, Will was there to help me unload my bags of clothes into the bin. Will even helped me sort through my recycled items in put them into their respective bins. It seems that I was always seeing Will help someone else.

Will was a diligent worker, despite certain infirmities. His eyes were not exactly focused in the same direction and his arm had a permanent bend in it, much like someone who might have suffered a stroke, and he had an irregular gait to his walk. It also seemed like he often had cuts and bruises on him, like he might have fallen or bumped against objects on a regular basis. But none of these things kept Will from catching the bus and getting to work every day. If Will missed the bus, he walked. I am not sure how many miles it was, but he got there.

The employees in Kroger spoke of Will's kindness. They said Will would clip out coupons and give them to the employees.

A few months ago, Will was hit by a car and he never quite recovered. This last week, Will passed away. He was not old by any means. I would guess that he was in his thirties or forties. There was no fanfare at his passing, not even a service for the community. I understand that he was cremated and that was the end of a life.

I am not sure why, but his passing has hit me hard. I wanted to shout out to everyone, "Look, look, at this wonderful person!" He might have seemed like a "least of these," but he made a difference. He had value and worth as a human being, and it was not a life that was lived in vain. He was one who was kind, compassionate, and gentle.

Will may not have been a community leader or have had wealth or power. I am not sure how much education he had or if he was a religious man. What I do know is that he was a hard worker, a helper to everyone, and that he was kind and knew how to smile. Those qualities made an impact on at least one human being. He did touch a life—mine. If Will did not know it in life, may he know it in death somehow. Thank you, Will, for being just you.

Prayer:

Father, we can all touch lives. We may think we are unimportant and even invisible, but we are not. We do not know who is looking, and sometimes it is a smile, a touch, and a work that touches another soul. Let us never forget, and may we all be servants.

Can you think of a least one "least of these" in your life? How have they made an impact on you?

_____

_____

_____

_____

_____

_____

_____

_____

_____

❧   THE PEOPLE OF MY WORLD   ❧

Proverbs 13:20
"He who walks with the wise grows wise but a companion of fools suffers harm."

I want to talk for a moment about the people of my world. Let me just say right off that they *rock!* They are happy, upbeat, positive, loving, non-judgmental, fun, and livers of life. I want to surround myself with these types of people.

If your life is like mine, then you have a full plate. My "free time" is very limited. I want to spend that time with the people who make my world a better place and make me a better person by being around them. I want to sit back and laugh or share in meaningful conversations and enjoy the beauty of God's creation.

I have learned over the years you cannot be everyone's friend. Sometimes you even have to sever a friendship that is no longer a positive influence in your life. When any relationship becomes negative or draining, one should not have to endure it. It is your prerogative to cut it loose and not look back.

I have heard that people come into your life for a season, a reason, or a lifetime. I have had a few in each category. I am fine with that. If I have to say goodbye to someone, knowing it is a forever goodbye, it may be a little difficult, but I accept the fact that the season for that person in my life is over. There are a couple of people who fit into that category in my life, and to be honest, their presence is missed in my life, and I dream of them from time to time. But they have no place in my present world. At some point, our roads took different paths.

The people of my world are of such good quality. They reek of goodness. They are lovers, not judgers. They help and don't mock. They know they are here for reason and they do not take that lightly. They care for those who hurt. They are the type of people you would want by your side or on your team. You could tell them anything and you would feel safe that they would never betray your confidentiality.

My question to you is, who are your friends and what do you do when you are with them? Is your relationship one that, when you leave each other's presence, you feel better because you were around them? Is there anyone you should be trying to cut the cord with?

Life is short, so choose your friends wisely. Do not spend one more minute with a person who brings you down, who talks badly about others, or is a negative force in your world.

Prayer:

    Thank you, Lord, for my friends. I feel honored to know them and to be part of their world. May I do my part to do the same for them.

List a few of your favorite people and explain what it is that makes them so special to you.

_____

_____

_____

_____

_____

_____

_____

_____

_____

❧ THERE OUGHT TO BE A LAW ❧

Hosea 11:4
"I led them with cords of human kindness, with ties of love."

I was recently asked to look into a camera and say, "there ought to be a law," and then I was to finish the sentence with what I thought was appropriate. The first thing that came to mind was, "There ought to be a law against mean people."

I have never understood why mean people act the way they do. In most cases, if you are a good communicator, you can calmly articulate your needs or desires without raising your voice or calling names. We also learn early on that it is better not to say anything if you cannot say something nice. The truth of the matter is, if we were to get in the habit of putting others first, our selfish nature would become nonexistent.

I have never understood what the big deal is about letting a driver over in front of you. I have never understood what good it does to give the poor store clerk what-for, for policies she did not create (like you have to have the receipt to return an item). I have never understood what good it does in a disagreement with a spouse to attack each other, rather than attack the problem. I have never understood what good it does to spread a rumor (even if it is a true one). Or why tease someone about his or her weight, hair loss, acne, clothes, or choice of mate?

When I see someone who is mean or self-centered, I just think to myself, "What that person needs is more of Jesus." (Actually my first thought is to let them know what a jerk they are being.) You see, the love of Jesus makes us more patient. The more we strive to be more like Him, the kinder we become to our world and the people in it. When we spend less time thinking about ourselves and more time thinking about what would Jesus do in this situation, we will become better humans.

Prayer:

Lord, give me patience for the mean people. Do not ever let me be like them. Help me to love and show even them how to love well. If not me, then who? We must find love for the people who are so hard to love.

How do you react to mean-spirited people?

_____

_____

_____

_____

_____

_____

_____

_____

☙ TIMES OF SORROW ❧

Isaiah 55:9

"As the heavens are higher than the earth, so are my ways higher than your ways and my thoughts than your thoughts."

It seems that tragedy comes in waves. I have so many people in my world who are currently hurting. A wife lost her spouse; a child is sick with cancer; a friend's daughter was hit by a car; a dad is dying slowly; and a couple's marriage is in big trouble. My heart is full of sorrow for so many people. My day is full of thoughts and prayers for them all. The focus is off of me. I cannot even begin to think of myself for a moment. I become unimportant. My worries become trivial. I am fully aware of the value of life. I pray for all of the hurting hearts and the wounded spirits. I thank God for all of my blessings and feel somewhat guilty that I have it so good when other people seem to have it so difficult right now.

I do not understand why husbands die and children get cancer. I cannot begin to understand God, but in my heart

I know God is in control and He knows what He is doing. I just pray for a big Band-Aid and more love and healing. I know God is good. I know life on Earth is not anything like life in heaven, so I will just trust. With a heavy heart and a quiet resolve, I hold my friends close today.

Prayer:

Father, it rains on the just and the unjust, so I hear. Life is not made up of everyone living healthy lives until they are old and then dying in their sleep. Father, I ask you to hold my loved ones close today. Squeeze them tight enough to let them know that you are there. Store their tears in a bottle so one day you can show them and say, "See, I saw them all." Be the Father of comfort today.

Do you ever feel confused about why bad things happen to good people? What is your answer to that question?

_____

_____

_____

_____

_____

_____

_____

_____

_____

☙ WALKING THE WALK ❧

1 Peter 4:10
"Each one should use whatever gift he has received to serve others, faithfully administering God's grace in its various forms."

A dear friend of mine asked me to read something the other day that I found rather peculiar. It was an obituary. Being that I am still a spring chicken, I have yet to acquire a taste for the morbid task of reading about those who are no longer with us. I reluctantly sat down and began to read about the life of an eighty-three-year-old man named Newton Metzger.

I could tell immediately that this man was a leader and had a servant's heart. He had served as chairman of the Wesley Memorial United Methodist Church building committee; he organized the local chapter of Gideon's International and served as its first president. He chaired the community's first United Way drive and served on the advisory board of the Salvation Army. He was also selected by his peers as the Rotarian of the Year.

However impressive all this seemed, perhaps Newt's most fitting epitaph was his own words, spoken in his last interview for the local paper: "The best way to live is to help someone else live more abundantly." Wow! That spoke volumes to me because the friend who had me read this obituary had reminisced to me on several occasions about this man who was so instrumental in shaping his life. My friend had lost his father in his early teenage years and was in much need of a mentor. That is when Newt stepped in, and he became so much more. He was a father figure who never ever criticized. He was a big brother who gave chance after chance to do better and succeed. But most importantly, he was an example, always maintaining the highest level of excellence and unselfishness.

For the next fifteen years, Mr. Metzger offered employment opportunities ranging from catching chickens to helping put out real estate signs, to helping with insurance collections. He taught my friend about working hard to be an entrepreneur. He taught the skills needed to get ahead in life, which is just what my friend did. My friend became very successful, and outside of his mother, Newt was the person who influenced his life the most after his father's death. He is indeed living proof that Newt's life purpose was served well and changed the life of a young man learning from a willing servant. I call this walking the walk, not just talking the talk.

I am thankful for both men whose lives miraculously entwined, producing two good humans that I am sure the Father is proud of, as am I.

Prayer:

Father, thank you for sending such a godly man into the life of a little fellow who needed an example like Newt. Thank you for one person's willingness to invest time, energy, money, and love into the life of another. Newt certainly was a reflection of your love and an example for us all.

Name one person in your life who walks the walk. What example does he or she set for you?

_____

_____

_____

_____

_____

_____

_____

_____

_____

_____

cs   WHAT MATTERS MOST   &

1 Thessalonians 5:15
"Make sure nobody pays back wrong for wrong, but always try to be kind to each other and to everyone else."

Does religion seem too difficult for you? Are you one of those confused souls who feel you just cannot live up to God's standards, so you are not even going to try? You feel too ordinary. You cannot think of a single talent or gift you possess. You certainly are not a public speaker if praying out loud to yourself is scary. Your voice was never meant to sing in the shower, much less the choir. You may have never been much in the leadership department either. You could never lead a Sunday school class or small group. You tried reading the Bible but got stuck at the begats. You tried praying at night but fell asleep before you could think of exactly what you should pray for. You would tithe, but you always seem short on funds. So there you stand, empty-handed, thinking to yourself, "Just what would God want me for? I have nothing to offer or sacrifice."

Are you ready for some good news? Jesus looks at us and says, "Hey guys, guess what? I want kindness more than I want animal sacrifices" (Matthew 9:13). He also said *"And what does the Lord require of you but to do justice, to love kindness, and to walk humbly with your God?"* (Micah 66:8). How about Titus 3:5: *"He saved us, not because of righteous things we have done, but because of His mercy."* Even Mohamed chimed in with *"A man's true wealth is the good he does in the world."*

What I am trying to tell you is that in you is the power to be kind. Do you realize that is the second greatest commandment: *to love your neighbor as yourself?* Stop believing the lie that you have to be Mother Teresa or Billy Graham to be worthy of God's love. You are called to kindness. Can you do that? If so, God will shine His face upon you. Sounds too simple, doesn't it?

Would you be willing to plant that seed of thought and water it? Try it and see what grows. Give it a chance. What do you have to lose but old thoughts that weigh you down?

Prayer:

Father, may this seed of truth take root in the heart of every man. I pray for a kinder nation, society, neighborhood, and most of all self!

List five things you could do that would be random acts of kindness.

_____

_____

_____

_____

_____

_____

_____

_____

_____

☙ WILD, WILD WEST ❧

Psalms 118:24
"This is the day the Lord has made; let us rejoice and be glad in it."

I should have been born back in the days of the wild frontier. I would have loved to be a little Indian girl. The thought of sleeping in a teepee at night, or maybe just under the stars, is appealing to me. To rise up in the morning and go to the creek to bathe or watch the sunrise sounds heavenly.

Let's get one thing straight, though: I would not want to be bothered with the "women's work." No sewing of the hides or cooking the buffalo for me. I would want to hop on my trusty pretty pinto, holding tightly to her mane as we tear out over the plains. We would spend hours exploring the boundaries of our camp. I would want to learn the ways of the hunter or scout. I would not even mind productive labor chores like taking down camp when relocating.

I just love being outside so much. I think that is why I see myself as Pocahontas (though my parents called me

Ellie Mae). When camping, I love sleeping outside by a fire rather than under a shelter. I like chopping my own firewood and often exploring my environment alone. I feel right at home in the nature that I love.

I now have a home in the woods that is secluded and private, and every day when I wake, the first thing I do is get up and have a cup of hot chocolate. Then I go outside and sit with the birds, and I watch the day come to life! I cannot thank God enough for the beauty of His creation.

If you could be born at any other time, when would it be? Can you think of qualities that you have that would be conducive to living during that time period? Allow your mind to wander there just for fun. Find joy in the qualities that make you unique in this world.

Prayer:

Father, I know you exist when I look outside. I long to fellowship with you the moment I walk out of my house. There is so much beauty in the world. I can see heaven on Earth when I am in the mountains. I am at peace in my soul. Lord, the cicadas are singing your praises this morning and so am I!

What time in history would you like to have lived in?
What would your role be?

_____

_____

_____

_____

_____

_____

_____

_____

_____

☙ **WINGS TO SOAR** ❧

Isaiah 40:31
"...but those who hope in the Lord will renew their strength.
They will soar on wings like eagles; they will run and not
grow weary, they will walk and not be faint."

Knowing that life is a journey, not a destination, really
helps me to put things into a proper prospective. Every day
I am alive, I want to realize that I am not under pressure
to hurry and arrive at some destination, but rather to just
enjoy each day and all that it has to offer.

One thing I find amazingly funny about my days on
this planet is I never really know what the day is going
to hold. One day I am soaring above the discord and feel
untouchable when it comes to temptations or worries. I
seem to have wings and soar above it all, and I just fly.
Then the next day comes and something happens. I falter
somehow. I am flat on my back and looking up at all the
other soaring souls and think, how in the world did I get
here?

The good news is, if you have ever soared, you will do *anything* to get back to that place. Soaring is the only place you'll want to be. Anything short of that feels like failure. It feels so much less than what we were created to do. God gives us everything we need to be free. He has a mighty hand to protect us, to lift us up, to carry us when we are tired, and to push us. He has in His toolbox a love so amazing that it is the only tool He needs. As a parent, He loves us without reserve and unconditionally. He loves us so passionately that we can almost get off the ground just from the butane that His fiery love emanates.

His one possession is success. We cannot fail. He took care of that, like a debt He has already paid. We cannot wallow around in failure. He says, "Get up, go on. I took care of that for you, now shake it off and fly...soar...be free." Flying with the Father—now that is the best!

Prayer:

Lord, how that feeling keeps me in check. When I am not in the clouds with you, I know something is wrong. My relationship with you is the thing that I value most in life. Thank you for the wings you have given each of your children. Teach us how to use them.

What would it take for you to spread your wings and soar?

_____

_____

_____

_____

_____

_____

_____

_____